Dirty Furniture

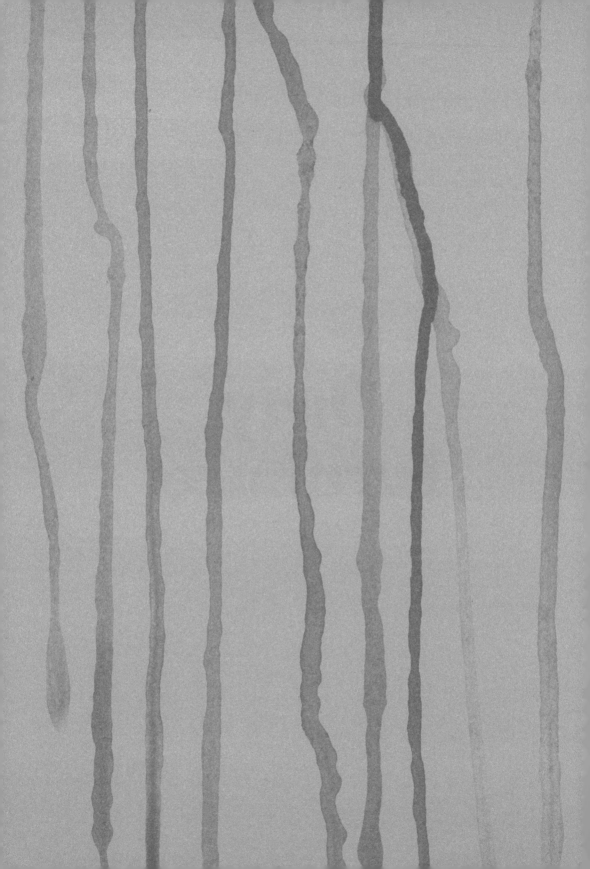

Contents

15 **Editorial**

16 **Anecdotes**
including *A View from the Throne, Latrinalia* and *Poo Protests*

30 **Architecture**
Public Inconvenience
Owen Hatherley

40 **Japan**
In Praise of Privacy
Julian Worrall

52 **Interview**
A Dairy Farmer

54 **Fiction**
Before Pudding
Rosanna Mclaughlin

62 **Photoessay**
The Grand Tour
Barbara Penner

76 **Humour**
Pull My Finger
Justin Clemens

86 **Interview**
An Engineer

88 **Visual Culture**
The Soft Sell
Alice Twemlow

98 **Gender**
A Piss-Poor Performance
Alex Schweder

110 **Interview**
A Paleoscatologist

112 **Visual Essay**
Power Toilets
Superflex

122 **Nappies**
Should We All Wear Nappies?
Natalie D Kane

136 **India**
A National Blockage
Debika Ray

The best inspiration source for contemporary interiors

Biennale **INTERIEUR** 2016

interieur.be

25th Silver Edition
14-23 October   Kortrijk, Belgium

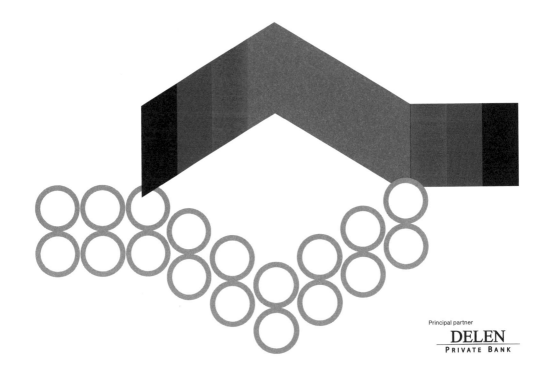

designjunction

> Immersed in design
22–25 September 2016
Granary Square
King's Cross, London

Register now. Please visit → thedesignjunction.co.uk

LAUFEN

A REVOLUTIONARY CERAMIC MATERIAL   SAPHIRKERAMIK, A HIGH-TECH
MATERIAL DRIVING INNOVATIVE DESIGN. WITH ITS PRECISE, THIN-WALLED
FORMS AND TIGHT-EDGE RADII, LAUFEN BRINGS A NEW LANGUAGE TO
BATHROOMS. COLLECTION VAL, DESIGN BY KONSTANTIN GRCIC.

COLLECTION VAL
Design by Konstantin grcic

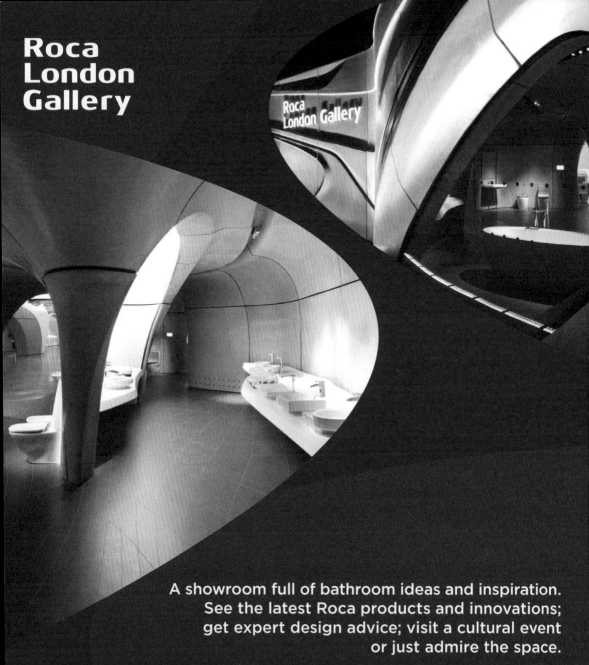

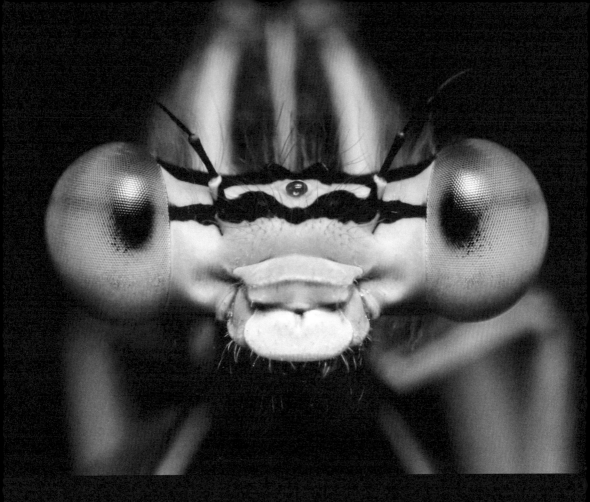

An eye for detail...
and a passion for print.

Park Communications   London
Beautiful printing   Award winning customer service

Twentieth and Twenty First Century Collectible Design

Nov 30–Dec 4/
Meridian Avenue & 19th Street, Miami Beach, USA/
designmiami.com
@DesignMiami   #DesignMiami

Design/
Miami/

Dirty Furniture

Editors
Anna Bates
Elizabeth Glickfeld

Deputy Editor
Peter Maxwell

Picture Research
Skye Arundhati Thomas
Rebekah Harbord

Creative Directors
Sara De Bondt
Mark El-khatib

Printing
Park Communications

Advertising, Sponsorship and Distribution
info@dirty-furniture.com

Cover Image
Anton Hjertstedt

Typefaces
Plak by Paul Renner
Plantin by Frank Hinman Pierpont

ISBN
978-0-9933511-2-9

ISSN
2055-7051

Published
Dirty Furniture
London, September 2016

Contact
editors@dirty-furniture.com
www.dirty-furniture.com
🐦 @dirty_furniture

Thank You
Rob Alderson, Brompton Design District, Jane Norris and our Toilet Break debates speakers: Jo-Anne Bichard, Shumi Bose, Pete Codling, Fernanda Costa, Alexandra Daisy Ginsberg, Owen Hatherley, Natalie D Kane, Gail Ramster and Cat Rossi.

Submissions
We're always looking for interesting stories and projects. Please email the editors if you have a proposal for one of our future issues: Closet, Telephone and Bed, and tell us a bit about yourself.

Subscribe
Buy the set or single issues online at www.dirty-furniture.com

Distribution
UK
Central Books
magazines@centralbooks.com

Europe and USA
Idea Books
idea@ideabooks.nl

Australia and New Zealand
Perimeter Books
hello@perimeterdistribution.com

Rest of World
Please contact us directly at
info@dirty-furniture.com

Contributors

Nadine Botha is a writer, curator, editor and poet from South Africa, currently completing an MA at Design Academy Eindhoven. She has written about design, art and culture for publications including *The Financial Times*, *Metropolis*, *DAMn*, *Design Observer*, *Dazed*, *Design Indaba*, *Mail & Guardian*, *City Press* and *Art Africa*.

Justin Clemens is an Australian academic known for his work on psychoanalysis, Alain Badiou, European philosophy and contemporary Australian art and literature. He is Associate Professor in the School of Culture and Communications at the University of Melbourne. Books include *Psychoanalysis is an Antiphilosophy* (2013) and *Lacan, Deleuze, Badiou* (2015) with A.J. Bartlett and Jon Roffe. He is also a published poet and contemporary art critic.

Owen Hatherley is a British architecture critic. He writes regularly for *The Architects' Journal*, *Architectural Review*, *Dezeen*, *The Guardian*, *The London Review of Books* and *New Humanist*, and is the author of several books including *Militant Modernism* (2009), *A Guide to the New Ruins of Great Britain* (2010), *A New Kind of Bleak: Journeys through Urban Britain* (2012) and *The Ministry of Nostalgia* (2016).

Arne Hendriks is an artist, educator and exhibition maker based in Amsterdam. His work is known for its radical ecological approach; projects include *Fatberg*, *The Incredible Shrinking Man*, *8 Billion City*, *The Academy of Work*, *Instructables Restaurant* and *Repair Manifesto*.

Anton Hjertstedt is a freelance illustrator currently based in the UK. His 3D renders evolve from thoughts of the abstract, rude and plain bizarre. His clients include *The New York Times*, *Die Epilog* and *It's Nice That*.

Natalie D Kane is a curator, writer and researcher working at the intersection of culture, technology, design and futures. She is curator and editor at Manchester arts festival FutureEverything and holds a research position at futures research lab Changeist.

Rosanna Mclaughlin is a London-based writer and curator. She co-ran a gallery in a flat in Balfron Tower, and her essays, art criticism, interviews and reviews have featured in publications including *BOMB*, *Frieze* and *The White Review*. She is currently establishing the publisher Twins Editions, which will focus on queer and feminist writing.

Jane Norris is transcribing postdoctoral research on Polychronic Objects at the Royal College of Art in London. She writes the 'Alphabet of Craft' column for *Crafts Magazine*, and regular opinion pieces for *Fiera*. She has presented papers at the Design Research Society Conference, Making Futures Conference and Research Through Design.

Barbara Penner is senior lecturer at the Bartlett School of Architecture, UCL. She is author of *Bathroom* (2013), and co-editor of *Ladies and Gents: Public Toilets and Gender* (1992). She is a columnist for the architectural journals *Places* and *Architectural Review*.

Debika Ray is a journalist, writer and editor with a background in international development and a specific interest in the Indian subcontinent. Currently senior editor at *Icon*, she has written about India for various publications including the *Guardian*, *Al Jazeera*, *New Internationalist* and *The Caravan*.

Alex Schweder is an artist who works with architecture and performance. Projects include *Practise Architecture* at Tate Britain, *Flatland* at New York's Sculpture Center, *Its Form Follows Your Performance* at Berlin's Magnus Muller and *A Sac of Rooms All Day Long* at the San Francisco Museum of Modern Art. Schweder has been a guest professor at the Southern California Institute of Architecture, Pratt Institute, and the Institute for Art and Architecture in Vienna.

Superflex is an artist group founded in 1993 by Bjørnstjerne Reuter Christiansen, Jakob Fenger and Rasmus Nielsen. Their works challenge power structures and relate to economics, copyright law and self-organisation. They have had solo exhibitions internationally, participated in art and design biennials and their works are represented in major institutions.

Alice Twemlow is co-head of the MA in Design Curating and Writing at Design Academy Eindhoven and the founding chair of the MA in Design Research, Writing and Criticism at the School of Visual Art in New York. Her book *Sifting the Trash: A History of Design Criticism* will be published by MIT Press in Spring 2017.

Sarah Vanbelle is an Antwerp-based illustrator and designer who crafts images with geometric shapes. Her illustrations regularly appear in magazines including *Monocle* and *The Wall Street Journal*. Her personal work has been published in risographed zines and she has exhibited internationally.

Julian Worrall is an Australian architect and writer, and Associate Professor of Architecture and Urban Design at the University of Adelaide. His area of expertise is in the architecture and urbanism of contemporary Japan. Books include *21st Century Tokyo: A Guide to Contemporary Architecture* (2010). Recent exhibitions and publications include *A Japanese Constellation* (2016) and *Eastern Promises: Contemporary Architecture and Spatial Practice in East Asia* (2013). He is architecture columnist for *The Japan Times*.

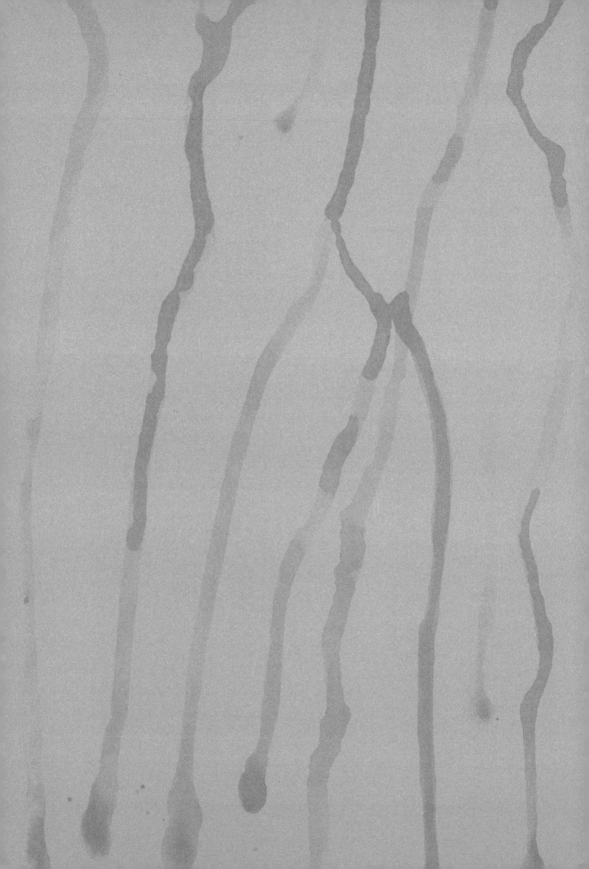

3/6 — Toilet

During the London Design Festival in September 2016, *Dirty Furniture* joined forces with The Shit Museum from Italy to present two exhibitions and a series of debates called *Toilet Break*. Our exhibition icon was the S-bend pipe. Invented in 1775 by Alexander Cummings, the S-trap was instrumental in separating humans from their bodily waste. Ecological theorist Timothy Morton writes:

> For some time we may have thought that the U-bend in the toilet was a convenient curvature of ontological space that took whatever we flush down it into a totally different dimension called *Away*, leaving things clean over here. Now we know better: instead of the mythical land Away, we know the waste goes to the Pacific Ocean or the wastewater treatment facility… There is no Away on this surface, no here and no there.

In this toilet issue of *Dirty Furniture* – third in a finite series of six – we attempt to straighten the S-bend and to confront our waste, to integrate the here and the there. In doing so we interrogate the future of this archaic device and analyse the reasons it has remained largely unchanged in over a century. Why do India's poor still prefer to defecate outdoors? Why do we insist on infantilising our bathroom products? Is accepting the genderless public toilet the only equitable outcome? What is the abiding appeal of toilet humour? And when did the nappy become such a contentious object?

Anna Bates, Elizabeth Glickfeld and Peter Maxwell

Illustrations by Sarah Vanbelle

LONDON, UK: Queen Victoria's toilet at the V&A museum is a fully functioning water closet. Originally installed for Her Royal Highness to use when she visited the institution named in her honour, the toilet is now available to visitors and accessed via a plain white door to the right of the museum's café. You approach it through an anteroom furnished with three heavy basins set in a cabinet. Opposite is a long marble top, solid enough to bear a royal staff and a brace of crowns. The toilet is in a generous but surprisingly simple adjacent cubical. This strange monument, lined with hypnotically monogrammed green and cream V&A tiles, offers a temporal portal, a palimpsest of empire amid the sterility of the modern toilets next door.

Sitting on her toilet I crumple the toilet paper in my hand, thinking of the folded histories present in this space. Queen Victoria – notoriously anti-feminist – pronounced that women would 'unsex themselves by claiming equality with men'. She would never have considered herself a cis-female given that for her, other sexualities, such as lesbians, 'did not exist'.

Avoid placing chairs or benches in toilet areas that encourage users to remain longer than necessary.

From *Designing Out Drugs Crime in Licensed Premises* (a guide for licensees, managers and staff) published by Hertfordshire Constabulary.

And anyway, as monarch, she was above all men in the Empire including her husband. Did she see herself as being above gender? Was she blind to the irony of her female status? How did this young woman handle the drug of power? In her tight conceptual cubical, Queen Victoria would struggle to accommodate today's sexual diversity: Cis, Trans, Bi, Queer, Lesbian, Gay, Asexual, Drag. If we had checked her urine from this toilet, would her sample reveal high levels of testosterone and explain her Empire drive? Was her gender warped through power? From this echoing, glazed, self-referential toilet she would not have seen the arrogance of her position. The monogrammed interlocking V&A on the tiles shout her propaganda of heteronormality. They fill my vision leaving no space to disagree: a colonial pattern replicated across the British Empire.

Historically to 'make one's toilet' referred to the process of dressing. It also alluded to preparation for execution, especially by guillotine. Power and toilets have always been intimately linked: they encapsulate the struggle between control and vulnerability. Contemporary designs for school toilets place doors at each end of the toilet corridor in order to prevent dead ends, and with that, bullying. Queen Victoria's military strategists might have benefited from this insight. The Indian Jallianwala Bagh massacre in 1919 at Amritsar in the Punjab was the result of British Colonel Dyer trapping unarmed men, women and children in a park with no way to obey commands for dispersal. Women jumped into the park cistern – to their deaths. This marked the beginning of Indian independence. As self-titled 'Empress of India' Queen Victoria viewed her role as propagating Civilisation. She would have been proud of Thomas Twyford's first ceramic British

Slavoj Žižek on toilets and ideology

And here, I came to think

of the toilets in America, France and Germany,

They make up a semiotic triangle that correlates exactly

toilet produced in 1883, oblivious to the fully flushing wet toilets of the Punjabi Harappan settlements from 2500 BC.

I tear off another piece of toilet paper and screw it up. The creases resemble a map, perhaps of the British Empire. Is this what Queen Victoria did in her rare moments of privacy in this space? As I uncrease the paper in my hand, I think of my British grandmother, born in Lahore as part of the Raj, and the strange folding of my connections to Empire, history and sexuality. *Jane Norris*

Research shows that the less secure, flimsy locks are better on cubicle doors as drug users are made to feel more vulnerable under these conditions.

Latrinalia

SAN FRANCISCO, USA: According to a survey of European bathroom habits carried out by bathroom brand Ideal Standard in 2013, under-thirties spend on average one minute and 39 seconds longer on the toilet than over-55s. A possible explanation for this comes from an InSites Consulting report, published in the same year, which revealed twelve percent of American fifteen to 34 year olds use social media on the loo. The younger the demographic, the higher the percentage: according to Nielsen forty percent of eighteen to 24 year olds admit to checking their social networks in the bathroom.

We shouldn't be surprised that the toilet stall is a place to consume and produce media; its walls have served as a means of communication for centuries. One epigram, discovered in the ruins of the Roman city of Pompeii, read: 'I'm amazed, O wall, that you have not fallen in ruins, you who support the tediousness of so many writers.' Martial, the first-century poet, even lampooned a rival by suggesting: 'If you aim at getting your name into verse, seek, I advise you, some sot of a poet from some dark den, who writes, with coarse charcoal and crumbling chalk, verses which people read as they ease themselves.' It's possible this retort was taken as serious professional advice: in 1731, under the pseudonym Hurlo Thrumbo, an English author gathered and published what he

considered to be toilet graffiti's greatest hits in a book titled *The Merry-Thought: or the Glass-Window and Bog-House Miscellany.*

By 1966 academia found sufficient interest in the phenomenon to anoint it a literary category: *latrinalia* (coined by University of California Berkeley folklorist Alan Dundes). The attraction of this genre to ethnographers and English professors is clear. Toilet graffiti is a type of folk art, distinct from the literary canon. The privacy of the cubicle encourages people who would not usually engage in public displays of creativity, to become authors, correspondents and cartoonists. The makeup of toilet graffiti – aphorisms, jokes, illustrated doodles, political shibboleths, erotic solicitations, threats of violence, gang propaganda – provides an unfiltered snapshot of a particular culture at a particular time.

It only takes a slight shift in perspective to see how the above list matches that of various contemporary internet-enabled phenomena, such as trolling, memes, or hook-up culture. The anonymity of the internet parallels the seclusion of the toilet cubicle, except now we all have a view of the stall. The bathroom wall is the precursor to the chat-room message board.

This was codified last year with the launch of the Pooductive app, a messaging platform designed specifically for inter-cubicle communication. Pooductive users can adjust distance settings to choose how local they want their fellow defecators to be, and the app also has a global option for those who want to chat shit internationally.

Since Pooductive gained traction, co-founder Marco Hernandez has begun to work with charities to raise both awareness and money for communities that lack proper sanitation. He never mentions the sanitary dilemma of using a phone while excreting, however the app does feature an 'I'm wiping' alert button, presumably so users can put their phone down when things get technical. The marketing material reads:

> Think of Pooductive as a place of magic and wonder where people from around the world can anonymously meet to enjoy their time of zen, peace and quiet together, by philosophising, sharing ideas and playing games against each other.

'Philosophising, sharing ideas and playing games', Pooductive digitises what the toilet has always been: a public forum.
Peter Maxwell

CAPE TOWN, SOUTH AFRICA: When Chumani Maxwele took to the statue of British imperialist Cecil John Rhodes in front of the University of Cape Town with a bucket of shit last year, it was not the first time activists in the city had resorted to using poo as a means of protest. In 2014, anonymous guerrilla art group Tokolos Stencil Collective surreptitiously planted soiled potties at two art events to infest the gentrified spaces with what they described as 'the smell of decades of indignity and oppression'. Most significantly, a year earlier in 2013, the Ses'khona People's Rights Movement earned its appellation

and is flushed through a hole
at the front. This way

you are directly confronted with
excrement - and you can see

whether you have worms
etc. This is a German ritual.

'the poo protesters' when members flung human shit at a bus transporting the mayor, and dumped buckets of shit at the airport and government offices.

Poo is a potent protest tool in South Africa for a number of reasons. The 2013 insurgence occurred because of the sanitary conditions endured by those relegated to informal camp-like settlements on the outskirts of the city, where there are no private toilets. At best inhabitants share a rarely functional toilet between four households, and many of these are unenclosed, forcing residents to shroud themselves in a blanket for privacy. More common are the rows of cement-enclosed chemical toilets that service an entire neighbourhood. These are notorious for being rape hotspots, so to avoid them, residents use buckets, which they then empty onto vacant lots causing children playing there to become susceptible to infections. The government has responded by providing rudimentary portable potties, colloquially known as 'porta-portas' or 'laptops'. In this poo apocalypse, a spot of shit-flinging could be considered quite restrained.

But the phenomenon goes deeper than demonstrating about poo with poo. The sanitary conditions themselves are emblematic of wider issues. 'What happens when we treat humans like shit, when we turn human beings themselves into the abject, into the thing that needs to be expelled?' South African poet and cultural commentator Rustum Kozain asks the privileged ten percent of the South African population that is pushing the poor to these inhumane urban fringes. Kozain traces treating humans 'like shit' back to the 'cattle class' of the Atlantic slave trade when human beings were shipped as cargo, living in their own excrement for weeks at sea. The conditions served to distance slaves from their European masters, further justifying the slaves' subjugation. Since then, countless dynasties have used the fear of dirt and regulation of bodily functions to include and exclude people – the most notable example being apartheid's separate toilets for whites and blacks.

The fight for dignified toilets, then, is both a practical and symbolic move towards decolonising the system. As long as the City of Cape Town does not lay down pipes in informal urban settlements, both the settlements and their inhabitants – uncannily termed 'squatters' – do not officially exist. Waterborne sanitation – a prime instrument of colonisation – and still known as 'Britain's greatest invention', is actually one of the most wasteful and inefficient waste-management systems. That it is still regarded by the disenfranchised as a basic form of legitimation is evidence of this insidious 'sanitary imperialism'.

The shit hurled at Rhodes in 2015 was therefore acute in its symbolism. It kickstarted the #Rhodesmustfall campaign, aimed not just at dismantling a statue of a notorious British imperialist, but also the embedded racism and Eurocentric syllabus of the higher education system globalised

Toilet cubicles should be constructed to allow for a minimum 200mm space from the floor with a reduced top height.

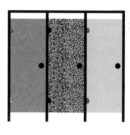

by British colonialism. The ceremonious shit-slinging sparked nationwide student protests, spreading as far as Oxford University. After twenty years of democracy in South Africa, higher education is still an economic privilege. Yet neither replacing waterborne sanitation infrastructure, nor rebuilding the university system from scratch, are going to happen; herein lies the bind of colonial power. Hence the recourse to shit. *Nadine Botha*

Courtesy of Independent Media

A protester throws a bucket of shit over the statue of Rhodes in 2015.

Anecdotes 21

UTAH, USA: A wide-eyed unicorn puppet sits as if on a chair and shits perfect swirls of rainbow-streaked, glitter-speckled soft serve ice cream onto a procession of waffle cones. A conveyor belt carrying the cones glides towards a handsome prince who takes one and licks it. 'The creamy poop of a mystic unicorn,' he declares in the tone of a superhero. For the next three minutes he invokes every pun that the current moment's penchant for conflating Mr Whippy with poo will allow.

Half fairytale kitsch, half infomercial, this YouTube video which went viral in 2015, helped triple the revenue of the company behind it. The video promotes a product known as the Squatty Potty: an unremarkable white plastic footstool that slots neatly around the base of a conventional flush toilet and which sells online for £27 a pop.

The science behind the altered toilet posture enabled by the Squatty Potty – obligingly demonstrated by the unicorn with the aid of superimposed graphics – is as old as man. A human's bowel motions are not controlled by the sphincter alone. A kink at the end of the colon, much akin to one in a garden hose, enables a build-up

Still from Squatty Potty video campaign
This Unicorn Changed the Way I Poop, 2015

of faeces until the decisive moment. This kink in our internal plumbing is known as the 'anorectal angle'. Standing maintains the retentive angle. Yet sitting on a toilet, as most people in the Western world have done since the nineteenth century, does not create a straight and direct passage. This only happens when our knees are elevated, as they are when we squat. Research shows that shitting from a squat stance is quicker and more complete; it prevents constipation, haemorrhoids and some suggest, even heart disease and cancer.

So why aren't we all squatting? The Utah-based company which launched the Squatty Potty in 2011 was not the first to advocate for a return to this toilet-going position. The cause was most famously taken up by architect Alexander Kira in the mid-twentieth century when he undertook seven years of painstaking research at Cornell University, combining fieldwork, lab testing and cultural analysis to consider the design of all bathroom fixtures from the perspective of the user. This resulted in his landmark 1966 book, *The Bathroom*. Kira's account of the benefits of squatting is as frank, rational and grounded in reality as the technicolour wonderland of the pooping unicorn is removed from it. The updated 1976 edition included a candid black-and-white photo essay of various squat positions with a human male model.

Today numerous devices on the market help retrofit the ubiquitous throne toilet to allow for squat evacuation: the Australian In-Lieu Toilet Converter and New Zealand's Lilipad work like the Squatty Potty; Nature's Platform (USA) is a folding table with a hole in it that sits above a throne toilet; in prototype, Jia Fang's Dyson award-winning Sit-Squatting Toilet Top makes the toilet seat a triangle to allow room for raised feet.

Courtesy of Squatty Potty

Yet the idea of squatting still meets resistance. The flush toilet and our position on it carries deep-seated associations in the Western imagination with civility and cleanliness; hence the tabloid headlines when in August, the Australian Tax Office announced the installation of squat toilets to accommodate its culturally diverse workforce. Kira too hints at why the return to squatting has not taken hold. Remarking that for many people (particularly the elderly) maintaining the squat is physically taxing, he observes 'the familiar casual "sitting-on-a-chair" posture so often assumed in a standard water closet, particularly by those who read there. In this posture the individual is essentially passive'. For many of us, time on the toilet is relaxing.

British industrial designer Pete Codling took such insights into account when in 2013, as a graduate student in innovation design engineering at the Royal College of Art, he set himself the challenge of designing 'a squat toilet for the Western market without the muscular difficulty and negative connotations.' He put his friends in various squat positions and documented their sensitivity to the slightest change in habit. His prototype, tellingly called Le Penseur (The Thinker), has a biomorphic, sculptural form. It elevates the knees by lowering the backside, supporting a squat but still enabling a relaxed position.

Working on Le Penseur provided Codling with an invaluable lesson in how to implement widespread innovation. After taking the prototype to international bathroom fairs, global bathroom companies and potential funders, Codling has, for the time being, shelved the project. 'The bathroom market is the most conservative,' he explains, 'The basic form of the toilet is something people

The French toilets have the opposite system: the hole

is bigger and at the back, so excrement can fall

directly into the hole and vanishes immediately.

are very afraid to change...The level of trust and commitment required to have a completely new toilet – that will forever alter your daily routine – plumbed into your house, is immense.'

The key to widespread innovation, according to Codling, lies in incremental change. He suggests, for example, that hospitals, gyms and spas adopt semi-squat toilets as models of wellness in order to facilitate their acceptance in the home. From this perspective, the £27 plastic footstool is a low-risk step in the right direction. Widespread change though may take decades to achieve. Until then, it seems, the return to squatting will remain a fairytale. *Elizabeth Glickfeld*

TORONTO, CANADA: That a café has opened themed around the poop emoji shouldn't come as a surprise. The new café, which opened last July, uses decommissioned toilets as seats, serves food in urinal-shaped dishes and features poop emoji murals. Somehow, the smiley poop has become one of the twenty-first century's most cherished symbols and one of the few emojis to have broken into the mainstream.

The rise of emoji has surprised their so-called father, Shigetaka Kurita. Working for Japanese telecoms company NTT-DoCoMo in 1998, he and his team designed 176 twelve-pixel by twelve-pixel symbols that would become the first emoji

1980s Japanese anime *Dr Slump*

Toilet roll dispensers, towel holders and drying machines can be purchased with smooth rounded surfaces to prevent drug preparation. Many companies now manufacture washbasins and urinals with sloping tops and sides.

system. The designs took advantage of the already engrained visual nature of Japanese language and communication. They referenced Manga comics – popular with all ages in Japan – as well as the Chinese characters of the Kanji alphabet, which often communicate through pictorial representation rather than through arbitrary signs.

Kurita anticipated his design would be a quintessentially Japanese phenomenon. Indeed emoji might have remained an 'oriental curiosity' were it not for Google, which, in 2007 made the decision to incorporate them into Gmail. Google worked with the major Japanese telecoms companies to standardise the symbols and, much to the consternation of the American juggernaut, their Japanese counterparts insisted that the poop be included; to them, dropping the poop emoji would be like dropping one of the letters of the alphabet. It's fun to imagine the scenes at Google HQ in California as harried marketing executives called high-level meetings to discuss whether or not to include a pile of faeces in their character set.

While relatively new to the West, in Japan, the rendering of poo as a pyramidal swirl of cream can be traced back to a much loved 1980s cartoon called *Dr Slump*. The animation featured pink walking talking turds with prankster personalities. Etched in children's memories and easy to replicate, the symbol was scribbled all over schoolbooks for a generation. A decade or so later (around the same time emoji appeared), Kin no Unko, or The Golden Poop, became a popular jokey keepsake, thanks to a pun on the first syllable of the Japanese word for poop, *unko*, and the word for luck, *un*.

In 2007, Google designers Susie Sahim and Ryan Germick revised the poop emoji, adding animated flies to its summit for extra verisimilitude. The shift to a more literal unpleasant rendering of poo, and its connection to dirt, moved the glyph further away from Japanese Kawaii – or cute – culture. In 2011, Apple swung in the other direction, updating its emoji set and investing the poop with human attributes: the poop now had googly eyes and a smiley visage. It was then that the symbol really took off in the West.

In Japan, emoji present a logical progression for a pop culture that pre-internet traded in an endless procession of replaceable cute mascots used to personalise uniforms, satchels and so on. Apps such as Line facilitate emoji-only communication, exchanges that are not literal but entirely dependent on context and shared visual and cultural references. New sets of emoji – now also animated – are frequently available for immediate download, to be consumed and circulated by an emoji-loving public before being quickly superceded.

Many in this endless stream of new byte-sized glyphs visualise bodily processes. There are farting cats, teddies on toilets and vomiting pumpkin heads. Writing about Japanese cute culture in *Eye*

Magazine, 2002, designer and animator Miki Kato explained this humour as 'the Japanese habit of self-deprecation. Japanese tend to enjoy funny topics for daily conversation, such as "what kind of dumb things they've done" or descriptions of their own mistakes. This is an attempt to disarm the listener, and to develop more intimate relationships.'

But something as popular as the poop emoji couldn't stay only on-screen. And so it is that the poop emoji broke into the physical world: you can now tuck into poop emoji cupcakes, pad around the house in poop emoji slippers and enjoy the outdoors with an inflatable poop emoji pool toy. Shit. *Elizabeth Glickfeld*

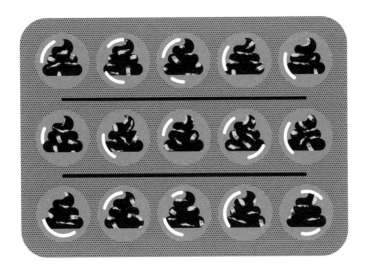

LETCHWORTH GARDEN CITY, UK: The absence of shit in medicine is relatively recent. Athenians used animal waste to treat sore tonsils, scorpion stings and flux. In India, cow urine was traditionally used to treat everything from heart disease to cancer and AIDS, and in China, flying squirrel droppings were used as a remedy for abdominal pains. While there is no medical proof that these medicines worked, they underscore a perception of shit, very different from the modern era's. In the effort to educate societies on the dangers of our waste, potential health benefits had to be washed from the public consciousness. But this attitude is beginning to shift.

In June this year, the Taymount Clinic in Hitchin, UK, relocated to larger premises in Letchworth to cope with the surge in demand for its miracle drug: shit. The clinic specialises in faecal transplants: a process whereby the faeces of a donor are watered down, blended and delivered into the anus of another person. Faecal transplants have become a popular method for treating *Clostridium difficile*,

a chronic bacterial infection that can cause long-term diarrhoea, fever, and if left untreated, death.

The science is easy to understand. *C. difficile* can be caused by antibiotics, which wipe out good bacteria as well as the bad. A dose of donor shit comprises 35,000 families of gut bacteria; once transplanted, these microbiota repopulate the intestines of the sick person with good bacteria, enabling him or her to fight infection. The treatment cures ninety percent of those suffering from *C. difficile*, and has also been used to treat other gastrointestinal diseases such as Crohn's disease, colitis and constipation, as well as neurological conditions. It has even remedied completely different medical complaints – unintentionally.

'My colleagues have certainly seen some interesting things along the way,' Emma Allen-Vercoe, a microbiologist at the University of Guelph in Canada told the *New Scientist*. 'They will perform a faecal transplant for *C. difficile* and then notice that…hey, they are not depressed any more.' Indeed, one of Allen-Vercoe's own patients grew enough hair to shave following his transplant, despite having suffered from alopecia since the age of six. With miracle stories such as this, it's no wonder transplants are catching on: at least eighty clinics in the US now offer the treatment.

The problem, of course, is that with the good side effects, come the bad. A patient of Colleen Kelly, a gastroenterologist at the Miriam Hospital in Providence, Rhode Island, for example, was treated for *C. difficile* using the faeces of her obese daughter and, around a year later, became obese herself – despite maintaining her healthy routine. As many medics have pointed out, the side effects could be much worse than obesity. In truth, specialists are still in the dark about what shit can really do.

The gut is a hugely complex ecosystem. The flora in our gut responds to everything we do and that happens to us, including our diet, antibiotic use and illness – and these are the influencers you can screen for. Emotional factors, such as the stress of an exam, moving home or the death of a loved one also affect our flora – but how do you test for these? Our guts are a physical trace of all our lived experiences. They document where we have been and what we have felt. Will these factors also be transferred when you take in someone else's shit? Artist Janani Balasubramanian thinks so. In her *New Inquiry* thought piece on the topic, she writes: 'The fecal transplant constitutes a transfer of the accumulation of other people's sensations and emotions from one gut to another.'

While the mind boggles at the implications of this musing, microbiologist Allen-Vercoe warns: 'It sounds ridiculous, but we can expect celebrities to start selling their own faecal samples.' Copying someone's style is one thing... *Anna Bates*

Toilet seat lids can be removed, but this may leave the toilets feeling 'seedier' as a result. Suitably shaped lids could be considered as a preventative measure.

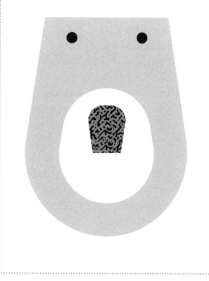

Arne Hendriks and Mike Thompson growing a fatberg

AMSTERDAM, NL: A fatberg is a large mass of solid waste in a sewerage system. Fatbergs form when cooking oil is poured down the drain; it solidifies in cold water and starts creeping up the sewer walls, like cholesterol clogging up arteries. Add to this the personal hygiene products we flush down the toilet, and you have a fatberg. Fatbergs entered into our imagination on 6 August 2013, when London's Thames Water Company issued a statement about a blockage of fat the size of a London double-decker bus, and gave the mass a name: fatberg. The BBC picked up the story and it went viral. Thames Water now employs a team of 45 'sewer men' to clean the almost 55,000 blockages a year, using industrial vacuums and high-pressure water hoses. Sometimes the rock-hard masses have to be removed by hand.

It was the ever-increasing reported size of fatbergs that ignited my imagination and that of my fellow critical designer Mike Thompson. After the double-decker bus, there were news stories of a fatberg the size of a 'hippopotamus', then one the size of a 'jumbo jet', and then there was a fatberg the size of a 'small village'. How big does fat have to get to make the news?

So we began constructing a floating island of fat. Situated on the old NDSM shipping wharf in the harbour of Amsterdam, the fatberg island is to become an autonomous space for fat to express itself and for the public to engage with. Why? Fat is one of the most interesting substances of our time: it stores energy; it defines our concepts of beauty; it is also a marker of our health. And never has there been so much of it: it is in our food, on our bodies (because we eat this food) and in our sewerage (when we throw our food away). There is a correlation between the fat on our bodies and the fat in our sewers.

We are defenceless to fat. It seems to want to express itself and is doing so aggressively, blocking our systems and making us obese. We have a connection to water: we use it, we drink it, we sail on it, we swim in it, we work with it and we manage it. So why are we disconnected from fat? For Inuits, fat is a source of life. What if we thought about what fat could be positively?

Confronted with a floating island of fat, we ask people to meditate on fat anew. Perhaps then, we can imagine how we might use its energy, and consider how we can give it new purpose. *Arne Hendriks*

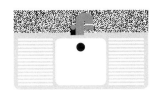

Avoid flat smooth areas that can be easily used as a worktop to divide and prepare drugs, or used as a platform for sniffing. Improvements can be made to flat surfaces within toilets by applying a rougher surface coating to these areas.

Photo by Hanneke Wetzer

their system makes most sense.
But clearly, a complex system

is at work here. And
if I am to carry on

of ideology, period. Yes,
but as soon as you flush

the toilet, you're right
in the middle of ideology.

Video stills taken from a Slavoj Žižek lecture given at an architecture congress in Pamplona, Spain.

Obnoxico

Not long after the Second World War, Richard Buckminster 'Bucky' Fuller, the American inventor, author and futurist, created a thought exercise to expose the ridiculousness of a market system that was increasingly manufacturing desire for objects of non-necessity, rather than real need.

He called this critical fiction – a hypothetical mail order business – Obnoxico. Its stand-out product? A gold cast of a baby's last worn nappy; a memento of the moment a child is toilet trained, in object form.

'The easily forecastable profits from this one item ran into millions of dollars per year,' Fuller told his students. But: 'You have to decide whether you want to make money or make sense, because the two are mutually exclusive.'

A couple of decades later, Fuller reflected on this project, in his book, *Critical Path* (1983): 'Somehow or other the theoretical Obnoxico concept has now… become a burgeoning reality,' he wrote. 'As the banking system pleads for more savings-account deposits (so that they can loan your money out to others at interest plus costs) the Obnoxico industry bleeds off an ever greater percentage of all the perennial savings as they are sentimentally or jokingly spent for acrylic toilet seats with dollar bills cast in the transparent plastic material.' *Dirty Furniture*

Public Inconvenience

The decline of the public
toilet has shadowed
the rise of global cities.
Architecture critic *Owen
Hatherley* considers the
implications of being
caught short in London.

In 1973, while working on the planning of the National Theatre, dramaturg and enthusiastic fetishist Kenneth Tynan recorded the following in his diary:

> During the night I have a dream in which I join a subversive organisation called the Socialist Lavatory League. Its purpose is to bring all private loos into public ownership. Everyone will have the right to use anyone else's loo – which will mean the end of private peeing. The dream wakes me up giggling, but on reflection I don't think it is all that bad an idea.

Initially, of course, the idea does sound absolutely ludicrous, but there are moments in the real world when something resembling it happens. Due to the inadequacy of the collected portaloos to accommodate the Red Stripe-drinking revellers making their way across W11, it has long been customary for some households to offer their private toilets to members of the public during London's Notting Hill Carnival, but being capitalism, the loo is offered only in exchange for a small fee. This scenario aside, Tynan's flight of fancy sounds increasingly plausible as a rallying cry, due to the progressive elimination from public life of something that was once a wholly normal part of urban public life: the public toilet. The Socialist Lavatory League could come into its own after the decline of the social democratic compromise of the municipal loo, leaving one choice: socialised toilets or barbarism.

There is no question that public toilets are a dying typology. Some cities have sold them off with alacrity; this has been a fairly predictable consequence of public sector cuts. The City of Manchester, for instance, has cut toilets so furiously since 2010 – an estimated 44 closed over five years – that there is only one public toilet left in this conurbation of over two million people (Mount Street, if you're wondering). A BBC report in May 2016 claimed that public toilets have been 'wiped out' in parts of the UK. Occasionally, protests are heard about this state of affairs, although usually people seem too embarrassed to express their opposition. The elderly in particular are widely considered to be the victims of the elimination of the municipal lav, part of their general excising from the public sphere in recent years (when was the last time you saw someone over fifty on an architectural render?). They're hardly the only people to suffer from the absence of loos. At this point, I should declare an interest, given that I have Crohn's disease, a chronic autoimmune condition that, among other things, manifests itself through exceptionally unpredictable bowel movements.

Public toilets at New Cross Gate, London

I know the counter-argument already. Ok, so pensioners and those with unpleasant illnesses might need this sort of thing, but the Victorian public conveniences being privatised all over London and Manchester served a purpose which is no longer really necessary. Like municipal bathhouses, they were a public response to the absence of private provision: you didn't need to go to the council baths if you had a good bath in your own house, and presumably, you don't need to go to the council loo if you have your own. Accordingly, public toilets are just pretty ornaments now. The buildings, with their attractive iron railings and moody sense of descent, can become all manner of things: one loo in Aldgate became a nightclub called Public Life, before going on the property market at nearly £1 million; another in Kennington is an arts centre known as the ArtsLav; and one in now loo-free central Manchester has become a swanky bar called The Temple. Similar to the repurposing of public housing as 'creative' space in Sheffield's Park Hill or London's Balfron Tower, it seems the public toilet is obsolete.

This is a dubious assumption. Usually Victorian bogs were put specifically in public places rather than in residential areas; they were meant to be used alongside private provision, by people who were caught short in the centres of towns and cities, when they couldn't get home to use their own. The result, across Europe in the mid-nineteenth century, was the creation of a new typology, part of a civilising process that also included sewers, underground railways, clean running water, the first non-market housing, and other things that private enterprise has never managed to do well. The most common London public convenience, which can be found in most districts and suburbs, features underground cubicles and urinals, lit partly through glass bricks, lined with wipe-clean tiles, and clearly visible from the street through wrought-iron signs reading 'Ladies' and 'Gentlemen', rather than the current, grammatically infelicitous use of the possessive pronouns 'Male' and 'Female'. These are precisely the kind of amenities most likely to be obsolete. Partly this is because of their widespread use for sex – particularly

The Attendant Café, a converted Victorian men's public lavatory in Fitzrovia, London

Bermondsey Arts Club, London

in Soho – and police forces the world over have supported the closure and privatisation of public toilets, on the grounds that criminal activity takes place in them with particular ease (to be frank, given the options of realising someone is being fellated in the next cubicle or becoming publicly incontinent, I'd choose the lesser embarrassment). The slack has consequently been taken up by two 'innovations', one being the single-person, enclosed automated toilet – an unlovely 50p-per-visit example of what writer Phil Knight calls 'the crap future' – with its clattering mechanisms, frequent breakdowns and perennial lack of soap. The other, less practical, solution is to use the nearest museum, café, pub or McDonald's.

The problems with the latter are obvious. In Germany, it is illegal for a building selling hot food not to have a publicly accessible toilet (oddly though, the need to use a privately owned amenity is less likely to arise given that it is much more common for the average U-Bahn or S-Bahn station to have a loo). Also, a toilet must be made available to anyone who asks to use it, according to the law. In Britain, however, cafés with fewer than ten seats do not need to supply a toilet, so your Costa, Caffè Nero, Starbucks or Pret A Manger may not actually have one at all, which considering the diuretic properties of caffeinated hot drinks is cruel, to put it mildly.

This might be about to change: the Greggs bakery chain was recently censured in court for having tables without toilets. Interestingly though, allocating space for tables instead of restrooms was not considered a breach of comfort laws, but rather a breach of those laws relating to competition. But the current situation is still grim. Should you find a place that actually does have a toilet, you will almost certainly have to buy something in order to obtain the handy code that you have to punch in before you can use the facilities. If they work.

I've had to work out a George Costanza-like knowledge of where decent public toilets are located in London.

In Britain, pubs can be easier, given the less harassed staff (in the daytime) and an absence of codes and locks, both remnants, presumably, of a continued belief in civilised urban life. Shopping malls, for different reasons, are similarly accessible, albeit frequently hidden in the depths of these increasingly labyrinthine structures; and museums are the best of the bunch, although of course there are far fewer of them. As for railway or bus stations, only the large hubs will

Helena Harry Design, Public toilets, RIBA, London

have anything much, and you'd better have the exact change ready. The tube, meanwhile, makes barely any provision at all. The Piccadilly line extension of the 1930s, and the Jubilee line extension of the late 90s are both peaks in London's public architecture, but even here don't get too comfortable: the Piccadilly line toilets are frequently closed and the Jubilee's amenities, while open a very civilised 24 hours a day, lack toilet seats, presumably an anti-vandalism measure; what you'll sit on is a built-in metal can, which is not pleasant in January.

As a result of all this, I've had to work out a George Costanza-like knowledge of where decent public toilets are located in London. Let's say you're caught short in the dead centre of town, around Piccadilly. Don't think you'll be able to use the toilets thoughtfully provided by London Transport in the late 1920s – as part of Charles Holden's remodelling of Piccadilly Circus – because like so many of the more civilised parts of London's infrastructure, they have long since closed, and now sit empty. There are toilets in another interwar structure, in the deco stairwell of Waterstones bookstore; and there are a couple of automated toilets off Regent Street. But if you aren't too desperate, by far the best option is to take the time to walk up to Portland Place, to the headquarters of the Royal Institute of British Architects (RIBA). They're just below the frosted glass stairwell of architect Grey Wornum's Mussolini-style Portland-stone cube; they're spacious, beautifully crafted and a pleasure to use.

Fittingly, perhaps given that they have probably the finest (semi-)public toilets in central London, the RIBA sponsored an open competition in 2009 for the design of a new public convenience, which featured entries from London-based architecture studios FAT, Eva Jiricna Architects, Will Alsop and DSDHA. On one level, this was an impressive project, given that the main surviving public loo in London is the faintly neoclassical automated pod – frequently found in Westminster borough and operated privately as City Loos. They exemplify some of the most irritating features of British public life: of course, the exterior has to be 'in keeping' – hence the pompous cornices and big royal crests – but in every other respect, they represent a chaos of privatisation and poor technology. Given they're one-at-a-time, they hardly help much with, say, central London on a weekend, and their coin-operated automated systems break down with great frequency. Back to the RIBA competition though, for which all of the entrants seemed to think, in a giggly English fashion, that toilets were *funny*.

Jiřičná is already partly responsible for one public loo in London at her Canada Water bus station; a miserable zinc and steel cubicle without a toilet seat. Perhaps because of this utilitarian precedent, she proposed brightly coloured cylindrical toilets, boasting video projections and vending machines, solar batteries, wind turbines and light sculptures, all of which seemed a little excessive for this most basic of functions. Other proposals were similarly ludicrous; among them a Cesare Borgia fountain, and vase-shaped pods. The statement accompanying FAT's grandiose design – featuring a gigantic head of Hercules and/or Athena – at least lamented our 'miserly public toilet provision', but as an act of satire: the Georgian toilet door resembled that of 10 Downing Street. What was most obvious from the contest was that nobody really took the competition seriously, using it as a pretext for sub-Monty-Python-like laffs. Not only did they think that toilets were inherently *hilarious*, but also, clearly, that their bespoke bogs were never going to get built.

FAT, RIBA competition entry, 2009

Park Hill Estate, an ambitious high-density housing development designed by Ivor Smith and Jack Lynn, who worked at the time for Sheffield City Council. Built between 1957 and 1961.

Before The Socialist Lavatory League becomes our only option, we should point to many successes in architectural conveniences. Among the many facilities, for instance, of Jack Lynn and Ivor Smith's Brutalist 'streets in the sky' in Park Hill, Sheffield, were the public toilets. Along with schools, shops and community centres, their design demonstrated an awareness that these needs should be accommodated by any viable social condenser, and also that people might come there who don't actually live there (currently considered by housing management to be the worst possible outcome). Alongside its monumental ziggurats, the Bulgarian seaside resort of Albena features a series of curved, barrel-roofed public toilets, as if Oscar Niemeyer had been given a commission for public conveniences. Some cities still have standardised toilets of a high quality: Iondesign's toilets in Alexanderplatz in Berlin are almost Miesian in their simplicity and elegance; and while the postmodernists who entered the RIBA competition took toilets as the opportunity for japery, CZWG's public toilets in Westbourne Grove are absolutely exemplary: civic architecture that is attractive and, crucially, well maintained, lined with green tiles rather than the zinc sheets that now seem obligatory. These are all comparatively rare, however, and that suggests something unnerving at the heart of the contemporary city.

Novelist Milan Kundera defined kitsch as 'the refusal to admit that shit exists', and neoliberal urbanism is based on a similar denial. We are to consume, but what happens at the other end does

Public toilets at the Bulgarian seaside resort of Albena

Architecture firm CZWG's public toilet in Westbourne Grove, 1993

not concern the powers that be. The infantile belief that toilets are funny, so glaring in that RIBA competition – the nearest thing we've ever had to a public debate on the architecture of toilets – actually assists in the denigration and disappearance of this vital public amenity, one which will continue to be important as long as we remain maladapted animals rather than disembodied consumption/production machines. Laugh if you like, but what has happened to toilets is closely related to what is happening to council housing, libraries and schools, and anything publicly owned that doesn't earn money.

Julia Baier, Sentō - The Japanese Bathhouse, 2005

In Praise of Privacy

Japan is famous the world over for its toilets. Architecture academic *Julian Worrall* tracks the squat's rapid evolution to the high-tech washlet.

In 1933, in his celebrated *In Praise of Shadows*, Japanese novelist Jun'ichirō Tanizaki writes:

> The Japanese toilet is truly a place of spiritual repose...
> No words can describe that sensation as one sits in the
> dim light, basking in the faint glow reflected from the shoji,
> lost in meditation or gazing out at the garden...The toilet
> is the perfect place to listen to the chirping of insects or the
> song of the birds, to view the moon, or to enjoy any of those
> poignant moments that mark the change of the seasons.
> Here, I suspect, is where haiku poets over the ages have
> come by a great many of their ideas...Anyone with a taste
> for traditional architecture must agree that the Japanese
> toilet is perfection.

There are many aficionados who would vigorously agree with the proposition that the 'Japanese toilet is perfection', but the toilet that Tanizaki was writing about so poetically is very different from what is typically understood as the Japanese toilet today: a technologically advanced tool for personal hygiene, replete with circuits, sensors, robotic nozzles and a remote-control panel. It is known as a 'washlet', after the product name belonging to one of its most successful versions. Tanizaki's toilet was a ceramic trench, addressed in a squatting posture facing the plumbing, located in an unheated wooden outhouse set amid the garden at the rear of the house, likely draining into a pit or septic tank. It is hard to imagine the tech-oriented enthusiasts of the robo-toilet consenting to a Tanizaki squat affair; for one thing, in such a posture your pocketed iPhone is in serious danger of falling into the mire.

It is striking how great the distance between these two images of the Japanese toilet is, and yet how both could be seen to embody an idea of perfection. For Tanizaki, the Japanese toilet was an emblem of tradition, taste and nature (elsewhere it was more commonly regarded as an undignified and unhygienic relic of backwardness). At the heart of these conflicting ideas of perfection are competing understandings of how you measure advancements in civilisation. This tension would underlie Japanese interpretation of their involvement in World War Two, a conflict seen at the time as a mission to 'overcome [Western] modernity' itself. Tanizaki's essay explored the idea that technology is culturally embedded, and far from being a neutral tool for the fulfilment of universal human needs, actually serves as an agent of cultural reinforcement and dissemination – and that much of modern technology was 'born Western'. 'Had we invented the phonograph and radio', he writes, 'how much more faithfully they would reproduce the special character of our voices and our music'.

An old Japanese squat toilet

Map of Tokyo, 1800

Although the flush toilet in its basic form as an irrigated ceramic chair is a Western import, the washlet – in its fully fledged configuration – is most definitely a Japanese invention. It would thus appear to realise Tanizaki's dream of a modern technology that embodies and upholds Japanese culture. But what precisely does this Japaneseness consist of? The irony is that the cultural essence of the washlet lies not in the supposed Japanese obsessiveness with cleanliness or technology, but in something more topical and universal: privacy.

In the Edo period (1603–1868), prior to the modernisation prompted by the traumatic encounter with Western societies bearing powerful technologies, human waste was a valuable natural resource – gathered in the cities by commercial nightsoil collectors and sold to farmers as fertiliser, greatly increasing their yields. Tokyo's celebrated Shinjuku district, inspiration for the futurist imagination of *Bladerunner*, was in the early twentieth century derided as the 'anus of Tokyo', through which the manure that fertilised the fields of western Tokyo passed daily. The ecological logic and resource efficiency of this traditional model was disrupted by the rise of modern sewage systems and flush toilets that channeled human waste into wastewater infrastructures, which before the 1960s generally did not have systems to treat the effluent, but discharged it directly into streams. Urban watercourses that in former centuries had run sweet enough to make tea with, were transformed into malodorous open sewers. The disease and nuisance that this provoked prompted the boxing of streams in concrete culverts, disconnecting cities from the waterways that had formerly been their lifeblood. Such were some of the retrograde effects that modernisation had on the urban environment. Ironically, the perceived improvements in domestic hygiene provided by the flush toilet were accompanied by an increase in water pollution and a worsening of public health – cholera outbreaks were largely unknown in Japan until the modern period. It is surprising to learn that even now, despite all the electronic futurism of the fixtures themselves, more than a third of the population remain unconnected to piped sewage systems.

Carts filled with night soil to be used as fertiliser, 1950s

Shinjuku Ohdori near Shinjuku Station, 1932   Shinjuku today

The consequences of the rise of the flush toilet – and its umbilical infrastructures – on the public cityscape are paralleled by the transformations in the private realm of the domestic interior. Facilities for bathing and excretion that were once independent and shared among a community are being progressively privatised and brought inside under the same roof. This is a story of the rise of privacy.

The public bathhouses, or *sentō*, were once the heart of neighbourhood life in residential districts of Japanese cities, their locations marked by little chimneys, puffing steam, poking out like periscopes above a sea of huddled tiled roofs with veiled entrances beneath a single neon hieroglyph glowing red, denoting 'hot water' – a sight that today is usually accompanied by a sigh of nostalgia. Bathing was a communal ritual, conducted nightly. (Their importance for community cohesion is underlined by the notorious tactic used by rapacious developers during the 1980s land boom to break resistant communities blocking development: buy out the local sentō and shut it down.) Meanwhile, the toilet, in the rented tenements common in the poorer districts, was a shared resource in the communal space of the residential block; while in the dwellings of the wealthy it was typically placed in an outhouse at the leafy rear of the plots, deep in the private realm. Spatially and

Torii Kiyonaga, *Onna Yu (Bathhouse Women)*, after 1780, woodblock print

socially, the bath and the toilet sat at opposite poles. An echo of this historical separation of washing from excretion is maintained in the typical family dwelling of today: rather than being placed alongside a bath or shower in the bathroom as is common elsewhere, toilets routinely get their own independent rooms.

However, the family dwelling is in decline. For over forty years, the fastest rising household category in Japan has been the single-person household. In Tokyo, this category now accounts for nearly half of all dwellings. This demographic shift has resulted in a proliferation of small apartments averaging 25 square metres in Japan's big cities. Such residences are typically serviced with a 'unit bath'. These are windowless one-piece rooms combining bath, shower, basin and toilet, seemingly stamped from a single piece of off-white plastic. With their unified materiality, radiused corners and tight dimensions, unit baths feel more like a piece of clothing than a room – a fully serviced and watertight inflated plastic suit that you wear by stepping through the door. They are made by the same companies that make the toilets (listed in the same product catalogues) and the qualities of the space that the toilet occupies – snug, introspective, secure – reach their acme in this unit form. Machined in automated factories, trucked to building sites, craned into place, and plugged into the plumbing and electrical infrastructure of concrete building frames, unit baths are the ultimate expression of personal space as mass-produced product.

Toto Washlet control panel and wand system

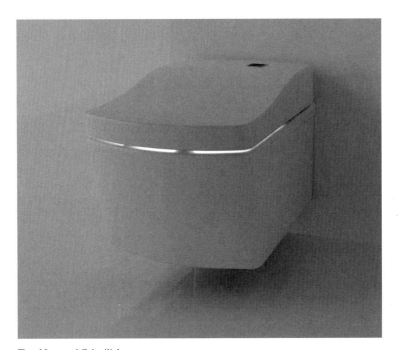

Toto Neorest AC Actilight

A typical unit bathroom

It is through this lens then, that the contemporary Japanese toilet is best understood: as the emblem of a society of mass privacy. Privacy is a distinctively modern concept, associated with a worldview focused on the individual rather than the family or the group, and as such was unknown in traditional Japan – as can be imagined in a society where houses have walls made of paper. Yet the recent rise of privacy as a core value in Japanese society has been rapid and forceful. The development and diffusion of the washlet has paralleled this rise. I suggest that the functional extensions and technological augmentations of the washlet can be seen as an outgrowth of the cultivation of the individual.

Credit for the invention of the washlet goes to the company Toto, which now enjoys two thirds of the market, with its arch rival Inax taking up most of the rest. In 1914, Toto's founder, Kazuchika Okura, was the first person in Japan to manufacture a Western sitting-style flush toilet; however, for many years these were only a niche product, with the majority of the market being for squat 'Japanese-style' fixtures. It wasn't until 1977 that sales of Western-style toilets surpassed squat toilets; three years later the first Washlet hit the market. Today, washlet-style toilets have penetrated over three-quarters of the market.

Toto and Inax are companies that take their leadership in the construction world seriously. In addition to continuous investment in research and development, both are vigorous sponsors of architectural culture, with ambitious high-quality publishing and curatorial arms. Toto Gallery Ma, in downtown Tokyo, is the most significant architecture museum in Japan, running a continuous programme of shows on internationally noted architects. It is both highly amusing and deeply satisfying to know that the exalted heights of Japanese architectural discourse are sustained by the limitless production of shit.

The contemporary washlet is the result of many iterations of innovation and refinement over nearly forty years, in both the design of the bowl and the seat. The evolution of the bowl has been driven by a progressive refinement in the flushing mechanism, to increase cleaning effectiveness and reduce water consumption, with contemporary tankless designs achieving a full flush with less than four litres of water. Sophisticated glazes have also been developed that minimise soiling. The bowl may be its body, but the washlet's soul is in the seat. This is the electronic platform providing the cleansing water-jet bidet function that gives the appliance its name. It is embedded with sensors that support an ever-expanding range of features and comforts: seat-warming; water-warming; blow-drying; deodorisation; bowl-lighting; music-playing; automated lid-raising and -lowering – all controllable by a remote or, most recently, a smartphone app. It is technically possible to flush the toilet while lying in bed.

Notably, in models designed for public toilets, the seat also contains amplifiers that generate a range of mellifluous artificial nature sounds, perhaps inspired by those Tanizaki so enjoyed. The sounds of a waterfall, ocean waves and crickets facilitate the performance of privacy. Clearly, public toilets present a dilemma for a privacy-obsessed populace. The need for silence and anonymity is constantly threatened by involuntary bodily noises that disturb and personalise this realm, intrusions that would normally obligate the voicing of an apology and a consequently embarrassing interaction between strangers. With the sound of water or white noise, anonymity is preserved and propriety maintained.

The contemporary Japanese toilet is a tabernacle of privacy; the washlet is its altar. Tanizaki's 'perfection' today consists of a hermetically sealed, technologically augmented realm devoted to the care of the self. However, there is one location in Japan where this reading is upended – a public toilet at Narita International Airport, the premier international gateway to the country. Here, Toto commissioned Klein Dytham Architecture to design a demonstration toilet space, to present washlets to

Dytham Architecture, public toilet designed for Toto at Tokyo Narita international airport, 2015

the world. In a typically irreverent twist, KDa takes the oxymoronic 'public toilet' as an opportunity to invert public and private. A video screen enclosing the toilet complex appears to project the shadows of the occupants to the spectators arrayed in the waiting area outside. Suddenly these shadow projections get up from the toilets and dance to unheard music, like denizens of old iPod ads. 'Come join us in the toilet,' these dancing shadows seem to say, 'it's so much fun!' Here the high-tech toilet becomes a vehicle for the optimistic projection of a fantasy future, in which toilets become public spaces of social gathering and collective enjoyment. Another vision of 'perfection' perhaps, indefinitely delayed.

Dairy Farmer
Gianantonio Locatelli

'The shit is more valuable than the milk.'

Tell me about your farm in Castelbosco.
I have 1,500 cows that produce milk for Grana Padano cheese.

When did you have the idea to start using shit as a resource?
Normally you just put the shit on the land. It is a good fertiliser, although it's bad for pollution. But the farm and the number of cows that I had were growing. I suddenly had a large amount of shit – the cows produce 150,000 kilos of dung a day – and this became a huge problem.

What did you do?
I thought, what if I could transform all this shit into electricity? I started researching. In 2005 I visited Germany, where they were pioneering the use of bio-digesters. In 2007 I started with the first digester. It wasn't common in Italy. It's expensive and there was no guarantee of results – so it was a tough decision.

How did it go?
It was not successful; I was depressed about the first results. The people working on it were not able to properly mix the best minestrone of ingredients in the digester – the recipe was wrong. I had to change the team and get the proper people for the job, and work with technicians, engineers, biologists, chemists…

How did you rectify the problem?
When all the bacteria are working properly you have the fermentation process, which produces the biogas. We added some corn silage – which we already had because it is part of the feed – to the shit. There was also a mechanical problem we had to fix, so it took a year to get significant results. When the first kilowatt came out it was a very satisfying moment. Since then the farm has been entirely powered by energy produced on the farm, and we sell the electricity we don't use.

How economical is it?
It's a big investment, but the system makes money; it's a long-term investment.

Would you encourage other farmers to re-use their animal shit in this way?
Absolutely, because biogas is the only renewable energy that works 24/7, 365 days a year – like a farm. And it helps the farmer make a profit from all the animal's activities.

Economically, how does shit compare to milk?
The shit is more valuable than the milk – especially because there are restrictions in Italy on how much milk you are allowed to produce. Now, the prices of agricultural products are very low so it's difficult to make a profit. Especially if you start with milk as an ingredient for cheese, then it's even more complicated because there's a chain; you have to make the products that help you make the cheese too.

How have people responded to what you are doing?
It's been a long process. It was hard to convince the farms around here you could do this with shit. In Italy there was a law against the use of biogas. But now it's working, people are convinced. Some Obama delegates came to Castelbosco to see this system. It's become a trend.

You have worked with artists on the site of the farm, and set up The Shit Museum, which tells the story of the farm and hosts exhibitions. Why the art?
Art is part of my background and art is fundamental to my way of processing and developing ideas; it's my driving force. Without the art I could maybe get to the point of producing electricity but not to the point of building the idea of the museum.

Were there particular influences?
I've been following art from the 70s… Fluxus…Pop art. Pop art is all about the transformation of something that is vulgar into something positive – the low becoming high – which is the idea behind this entire project. With the Merdacotta material we were trying to embody these ideas.

Can you tell us more about Merdacotta?
The process of extracting methane leaves behind a dry material which has a little part of straw in it. This is mixed with clay to make Merdacotta. It's like terracotta but it's lighter, and has a beautiful texture. The idea started when we were making the museum. We were already re-using dung to make the walls, as well as some experimental projects. But I wanted to do something more.

You worked with architect Luca Cipelletti to develop the range of products made with this material. Why did they take the form they took?
It was simply the idea of going back to basics – adding any other detail to the items would take away from the proper message.

What does the cheese producer that you work with think of The Shit Museum and the projects that you've done?
They like the enormous amount of communication! But they don't contribute to the project, because they have a problem with linking their cheese to shit. This is one of our next goals. We want to make a stronger link between food and shit.

Before Pudding

A short story by
Rosanna Mclaughlin

'Here's to Guy, and the brilliant job he's done on the place. Mate really, I don't know where you found out about half of this stuff but it's *fucking fantastic*.'

Guy smiled modestly in acknowledgement and surveyed the warehouse. Nine months it had taken to transform it from a storage facility for knock-off handbags, and into a home for his cousin Millie and her husband Seb. And Seb was right: it did look good. The polished concrete floors, the exposed brickwork. Bricks, which had been shipped from Guy's grandmother's summer house in Brittany – it had taken all his know-how in the family diplomacy department to talk Nanou into knocking down that old atelier – and which, on arrival in Bermondsey, had been grafted on to the existing breeze-block walls.

'My favourite thing down here,' said Seb, 'has to be those lights. They're completely brutal!' The two pendant lampshades hanging from the ceiling really were something. A pair of wide steel domes, their metal surfaces grazed with rust. Guy had bought them from a clearance sale at an old abattoir in Germany – mid-century classics he'd been assured – but the seller had been hazy on the specifics. Suspended now over the rugged, wooden table, they illuminated the party that had gathered for dinner: Seb and Millie, Guy, and Will, an old school friend of Guy's who ran Seed, a photography gallery under the nearby railway arches, and who had sourced the large photograph leaning now against the brick wall.

'Tonight is a very special night, and we're so glad you could both be here. Not only is the warehouse officially converted,' Millie said, raising her glass and eliciting a small cheer in the process, 'but it's also Seb's fortieth this weekend. As a treat, Guy and I have kept one room in the house top secret. The en suite loo on the mezzanine has been completely out of bounds to poor Seb for a month now, and I know he's dying to see what we've got in there. But Guy made him promise, scout's honour, that he wouldn't so much as peek.'

'And I've kept my word, haven't I Mills? But I must say, I haven't a clue what's up there.'

'You'd never believe me if I told you,' she replied, wrapping her arms around her husband's neck, 'because Guy's always been ahead of the curve. I'm going to embarrass him now, but I remember when he was a little boy and we were sailing on the *Octavia* – now, where were we Guy? That holiday when Uncle Bert had his moustache shaved off by that terribly severe local barber, when all he'd wanted was a trim.' Guy remembered it well, one of many Caribbean summers spent on Nanou's yacht. 'Yes, that's it, Turks and Caicos. Anyway, even though we were on the water almost the entire time – and when we weren't we were knee deep in sand or at the sailing club, and everyone knows how strict those old blazers can be – Guy insisted on bringing his skateboard *and* his turntable.'

Guy had changed in the fifteen years since that holiday, but not much. His eyes were still a bright, wet blue, only encased now behind tortoiseshell glasses. His cheeks were hollow where once they had been cherubic, but they retained the blush of the English orchard. His hair was a darker shade of sandy blonde – less Caribbean, more North Sea – and though he no longer skateboarded he applied the same distinction of care to his hand-built, bottle-green racing bicycle. Indeed, in recent months he had developed a fondness for keeping his bicycle clip around his ankle at all times – a sign of his indefatigable readiness, it also lit up terrifically well under UV (although Guy himself did not like to boast, he had it on good authority that when he flashed his leg out from behind the DJ booth, the sight of that clip tight against denim could drive a woman wild).

The door to the kitchen opened, and two young women dressed in black entered the room. They placed before each person an oak board, on top of which was a mound of pulled pork, some pickles, and three miniature brioche buns artfully stacked in a pyramid.

As the food was being served, Millie cast an appreciative eye around the room. Everyone had been so generous. The photograph Will had installed that afternoon – at over six foot tall and framed in raw steel, it had taken four men to place it in position – was the perfect accompaniment to the meat-hook coat rack by the front door. She looked at Guy's canvas workwear jacket, hanging from it now. That labourer look had since come into fashion, and even Seb had a camouflage number knocking around with his gilets in the wardrobe somewhere, but Guy had picked his up at a thrift store in San Francisco. An original, 1970s street-sweeper's jacket, municipal issue. An eye for authenticity, she thought, that was just so typical of him.

'When we started bouncing around ideas for this place, Guy said to me, "Don't you think design should be naked?"' Seb said to Will across the table, who nodded his agreement. 'And he was spot on. When you think about it, this country is going to the dogs – seriously, I read an article on it somewhere – the whole world is going to the dogs, because everyone has forgotten what it means to be human. I mean literally, how many people do you know who could hunt an animal and eat it? I'm talking about naked, red-blooded humanity.'

'Seb darling, where did you read that?' Millie chipped in.

'Oh, it must have been in *Lorgnette,* or *Nu-Gent* – one of those magazines. Anyway what the guy said was, utility is more than just fashion. It's what we eat, what we wear, where we live. It's a whole *lifestyle.*'

Seb broke off to prod at what remained of his pork, before sliding the unctuous, beige meat into the last of his miniature buns with his fingers.

'*God* this is delicious, Mills. So this guy got me thinking, when disaster strikes, and mark my word it will – when North Korea blows us to smithereens, or the polar bears land at Dover, and we all have to shoot birds from the pillboxes if we want to eat anything – who do you think are going to be the ones to survive? Not the magnolia walls brigade, *they* wouldn't last a single season. It'll be those who have learnt to appreciate utility. It'll be those of us who can hit a bird at sixty yards, train a dog to fetch it, and have a bloody great fire lit to roast the thing on.

So with this place, we decided we wanted to get back to choosing things because we need them, get back to finding the beauty in use. What was that thing you said, Guy?' asked Seb, sucking the juice from his fingers. 'Yes, that's it – *make function the boss of form*. Guy showed us some converted warehouses where the wiring had been pulled out of the ceiling so you could see it, so the colour of the cables and the brick were the palette for the interior, and not Farrow & Ball or any of that mumsy rubbish. Millie fell in love with these aluminium air ducts we saw at this conversion off Clapham Common, didn't you Mills? It was an amazing place actually, the couple who owned it had installed a wood-burning hot tub on the decking, and all the furniture was made out of vintage vegetable crates. Anyway, even though we didn't have any air ducts here – honestly Mills, you couldn't *buy* a better cousin – Guy arranged to have one put in anyway.'

They all looked up. A braid of rainbow-coloured electrical wire ran across the centre of the ceiling, to the left of which a metal air duct extended from one end of the room to the other, linking nothing to nowhere, but with a convincing affectation of purpose.

'Before we go upstairs to see the toilet Will', said Millie, 'we've been desperate for you to enlighten us about that photograph.'

Will turned towards the picture propped against the wall, and began to arrange his body in a manner that Guy had first seen in sixth form, and which invariably meant his friend was about to say something worth listening to. First, he separated his legs, so that his chinos pulled taught against his thighs. Then, as if he was simultaneously putting out two cigarettes, he slowly twisted the balls of both feet into the floor. 'I wanted the photograph to be experienced right here with you, not like a window into a different world. I wanted to break down that fourth wall, so that the picture is *in this room* – that's why I decided to lean it, to show all of it, be true to the object.'

The photograph in question had been the product of a lengthy selection process. Seb had wanted a Shibari print from Seed's last exhibition, but that had been ruled out as Nanou would be visiting in the spring, and she still suffered flashbacks from the time she got tangled in rope sailing *Octavia* solo off the coast of Dubrovnik (it had taken the lifeguard over an hour to unbind her). Guy had advised that it was probably for the best anyway, because as a rule of thumb, it's usually a good idea to buy artworks that you don't very much like. All truly profound works of art are ugly at first, and it is far better to learn to love something than to fall out of love too quickly. He had suggested instead they go for the photograph which stood framed before them now: a picture of a cardboard box on a gravel floor. The cardboard still bore the indentation of human buttocks where someone had evidently been sitting. A solitary weed grew out of the dirt, a cat – or perhaps a small dog, or else a dehydrated human – had relieved itself of two minute, lamp-black turds, and in the foreground an empty carton of cigarettes had been squashed into the gravel.

Will turned his attention once again to the task of extinguishing invisible cigarettes. 'This photograph is exactly about the essential beauty of the home. Even a cardboard box can be beautiful, and that crumbling wall is like a Rothko painting – its ambience, the way the colours fade out. It's like this guy, whoever the guy is that lives on this box, he's the lucky one.'

The reverie that spread throughout the room in the wake of Will's elucidations was broken only by the reappearance of the two women in black, who had come to clear the table.

'Ok Guy,' said Millie, 'I think Seb has waited long enough. Before pudding, will you do the honours and lead the way?'

The group followed Guy up the suspended staircase and on to the mezzanine. They passed Seb and Millie's bed, inset into the floor like a soft-furnished swimming pool, before coming to a halt in front of the toilet door. Guy snuck in for one final check, flicking on the light switch in the process, and a few moments later the door, after a month of secrecy, swung to.

The room inside was the size of a double bedroom, but it contained only two objects. A magenta neon light sprawled across the wide, back wall, like a drunken signature writ large upon the brickwork: illegible, but definitely profligate. Beneath the neon light, and bathed in its pink glow, was a stainless steel toilet. Seb and Will dropped down on their haunches like a pair of wicketkeepers: it was clear that this was no ordinary loo.

'It's like a pocket knife,' said Seb eventually, breaking the silence from his squatting position, his voice tuned tight by excitement, 'the way all the parts are combined in one.' And, after a fashion, he was right. Not only was the design remarkably compact, it had a potential violence about it too, which winked in the metal surfaces. The main bulk of the thing consisted of a broad, hexagonal column, fixed flush against the wall. Inset into the top of this column was a shallow sink, with a number of knobs populating the rim, and into its side a circular recess, with space enough for a single roll of toilet paper. And right at its base, no more than a metre from Seb's nose and practically kissing the polished concrete floor, was a broad, seatless, steel bowl.

'Where on earth did you get it from?' asked Seb. 'Nasa?'

'Is it vintage Scandinavian?' Will offered, noting its minimal purity. 'I have a Danish 50s dinner tray just like it, in steal and teak –

it has a separate compartment for afters. Or perhaps something from the Donald Judd collection?'

'Even better', said Millie. 'Happy Birthday, darling – it's from an *American prison*.'

Seb and Will's eyes dilated with disbelief, mightily impressed by such a find.

'Guy says they have them all over the States. That's why all the edges are rounded – so the prisoners can't prise the metal open and use the parts for weapons.'

'I bet', whispered Seb, who had lowered himself on to his knees, and was running his fingers over the cold, pink-tinged shaft in admiration.

Guy had first seen such a toilet installed at a friend's apartment in Manhattan earlier that year, and had known immediately that it was just the thing for Seb and Millie's conversion. His friend had bought his from a company Stateside that sells them chrome plated, but Guy being Guy, he was convinced that the original steel model was much more honest, especially if he could get hold of one that had seen the inside of a cell. And so, throwing caution to the wind, he had decided to do some first-hand research, hitching a ride to San Quentin Prison with a fashion designer he knew, who was out there working on a new line of boiler suits. 'He scrapped the idea of buying second-hand pretty quickly after that, let me tell you,' said Millie. 'He never got clearance to enter the prison, and the sanitation was so awful at the local motel that poor Guy was bed-bound and on a strict diet of Pepto-Bismol for an entire fortnight. In the end he had this toilet shipped new from the manufacturer in China. There have of course been some upgrades,' she said, tugging at Seb's sleeve and drawing him up to his feet. 'Press that button by the sink.'

Seb depressed a small, steel button, causing a fragrant gel to squirt out of a tiny hole and into the palm of his hand.

'Doesn't it smell good? Tobacco and cedar wood – Guy bought it especially.'

Seb rubbed his hands together and inhaled deeply. 'Mate,' he said excitedly, thrusting his fingers under Will's nose, 'I smell like I've been dragging hides across the Canadian wilderness!'

'But wait until I tell you the most amazing thing. Guy showed me – there are absolutely no joins, no fastenings.' It was true: not a single piece of hardware could be seen upon its surface, and the metal was completely seamless, as if the entire thing had been welded from the inside. 'And did you notice how shallow the toilet bowl and the sink are? You'd never manage to drown anyone in there. And there's nothing you can tie your boiler suit around either. It's completely *suicide proof*.'

Downstairs the table was being laid for pudding, and the sound of crockery drifted up to the mezzanine floor. 'Salted caramel ice cream!' said Millie. 'We better get a move on, before it melts.'

Outhouse, Alabama, USA, undated
The design of the modern bathroom is culturally determined and
historically specific. Traditionally, bathing, washing, and excreting
were done communally: they were sites of socialising – not of shame.

The Grand Tour

The development of the bathroom charts some of our deepest fears and desires. Author of influential book *Bathroom*, *Barbara Penner* takes us on a visual tour charting this important room's evolution.

Twyford, Unitas wash-out pedestal closet, mid-1880s

From the start, the English set the model and led the world in luxury bathrooms, arranged like furnished rooms with fixtures encased in fine wood. The potteries of Stoke-on-Trent produced a stream of evermore gorgeously decorated pedestal water closets, celebrations of technological and artistic prowess, which could be found from Argentina to Australia.

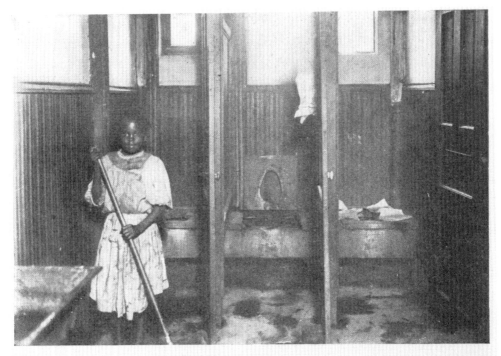

Toilets and a Tenant of "Douglas Flats," the Largest Tenement in Washington; Supposed to Have Been Erected as a Model.

[Photo by Hine]

Lewis Wickes Hine, Toilets and a Tenant of Douglas Flats, c 1908

From the early nineteenth century, in Western countries, these functions became individualised and architecturally segregated with walls, doors and locks. Such highly atomised arrangements are not 'natural'; they are reflections of our evolving ideas about civilisation, the body, decency, femininity, and sex.

GOOD HOUSING

GOOD ENVIRONMENT IS THE BASIS OF HEALTH

FULL EMPLOYMENT

GOOD FACTOR

Ernö Goldfinger, 'Good Environment is the Basis for Health', display board for Army Bureau of Current Affairs *Health* exhibition, 1943
In the early twentieth century, plain white bathroom equipment emerged as a resonant symbol of modern values, such as hygiene and cleanliness. The toilet became a symbol of modernity itself and the triumph of a culture of flushing.

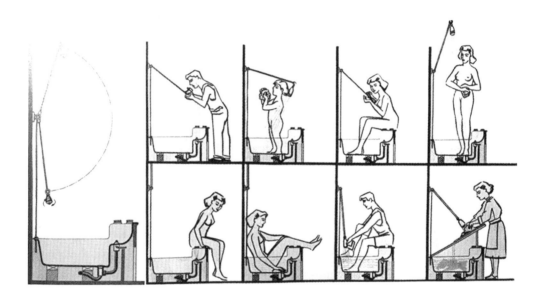

Bloc Poliban, L'Art Ménager Français, 1952
For the first half of the twentieth century, the bathroom was viewed as an icon or as a planning problem: how could bathrooms be planned most rationally to save on space and plumbing costs? The French-design Poliban was a miracle of compactness, an all-in-one cleansing station – at once a sink, bath, shower, bidet and laundry.

Jayne Mansfield, Pink Palace, Hollywood, California, 1960
In the postwar era, the bathroom changed. No longer dominated
by the functionalist, hygienic aesthetic, bathrooms softened and
warmed up, literally, with the introduction of plastics, carpeting,
and central heating. Once again, they became places of leisure,
sociality and sensuality.

Luigi Colani, bathroom series for Villeroy & Boch, 1975

The 1970s saw radical efforts to rethink how bathing and excreting might be accommodated – to make them safer, healthier, and more convenient. A greater interest in ergonomics meant that the design of bathroom equipment, especially toilets, began to respond more to the body.

Sanyo, Ultrasonic Bath and Washing Machine, Osaka World Fair, Japan, 1970

Japan led the way in many experiments to rethink bathing. At the 1970 World Fair in Osaka, Sanyo unveiled its Ultrasonic Bath and Human Washing Machine, a device in which users were soaked, washed with suds from ultrasonic waves, rinsed, massaged with rubber balls, and dried with heat lamps.

Courtesy of Sanyo Electric Co., Ltd

***Stop the Five Gallon Flush*, Minimum Cost House Group, School of Architecture, McGill University, 1973.**

The 1970s also saw concerns about water conservation come to the fore. The ground-breaking book *Stop the Five Gallon Flush* (1973) was an eye-opening menu of toilet technologies around the world. Low-flush toilets, toilets that used grey water for flushing, and compost toilets were all championed. Environmentalists and visionary engineers dreamed of 'closing the loop' – using human waste as fertiliser or as biogas, an alternate fuel source.

WATERBORNE

SPACEMASTER

Manufactured by:
Monogram Industries Inc.
Consumer Products Division
4030 Freeman Blvd.
Redondo Beach, CA. 90278, USA.

This vertical element contains a sink, shower <u>and</u> flush toilet in a floor space of only 9" x <u>23"</u> (22 cm x 57 cm). The toilet folds down from the wall, as does also the shower pan. The sink is permanently built in, and the faucets are also connected to a telephone shower. The entire unit weighs 36 lbs (18 kg) and is designed to be used in recreational vehicles.

MINIMUM SANITARY UNIT

Designed by:
Minimum Cost Housing Group
McGill University

A hand washing basin is combined with the toilet tank lid to make use of dirty water for toilet flushing. This also reduces space requirements in tight planning situations. The Minimum Sanitary Unit was used in the ECOL Operation. The only manufacturer we know of of a similar system is in Japan (see this page). Too bad.

TOTO

Manufactured by:
Toto Ltd.
1-1 Nakashima, 2-Chome
Kokurakita-Ku, Kitakyushu, 802 Japan

This large Japanese manufacturer of plumbing fixtures makes a number of flush toilets that are combined with hand-washing basins. Two models are illustrated here. The C730-S731B combines the basin and the cistern with a conventional toilet seat. The C750AV-S670B combines a corner sink-cistern with a water-flushed squatting toilet. In both cases the dirty wash water is stored in the cistern and subsequently used for flushing.

These type of toilets not only conserve water but also save space and reduce the cost of the fixture.

W+W Roca, combined sink and toilet that uses greywater from hand washing to flush the toilet, 2012
Efforts to redesign the toilet to make it more environmentally friendly continue today. In an age of water scarcity, can we continue to justify flushing an average fifty litres of potable water down the toilet every day?

Atelier van Lieshout, *Uritory* (a unisex urinal attached to a small biogas unit), 2003 and *The Eternal Flame*, 2008

Attitudes towards toilets remain conflicted. They are suppressed in polite discourse, emerge in euphemisms or jokes, and trivialised. But they remain fertile terrain for artists who use them to probe existing social taboos and envision utopian futures: why are bathrooms designed as they are? Could they be designed differently? And how might society be transformed if they were?

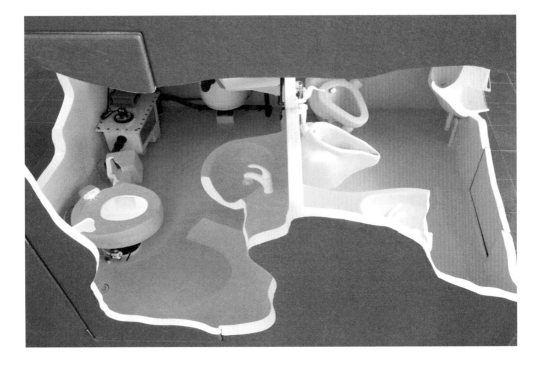

Pull My Finger

Everyone loves a good fart gag or poo-bum joke. Academic *Justin Clemens* psychoanalyses our perennial fascination with the one about…

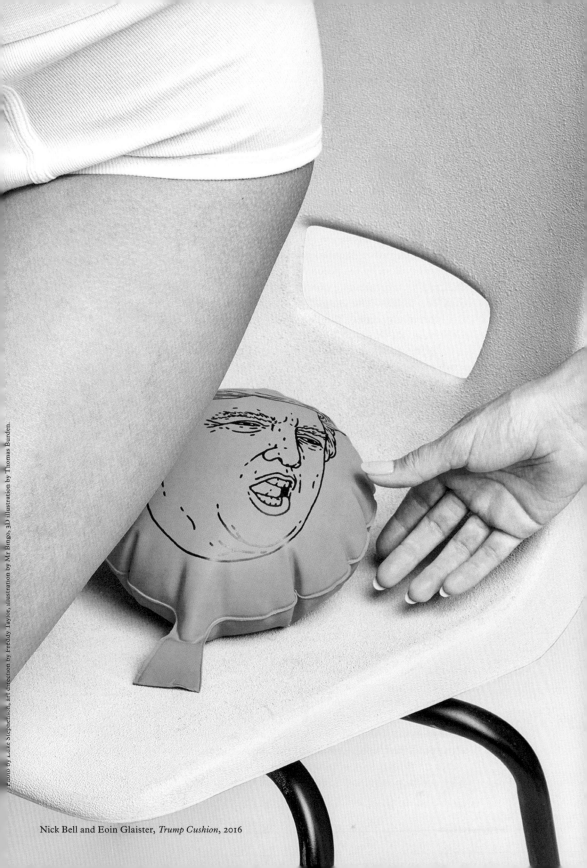

Nick Bell and Eoin Glaister, *Trump Cushion*, 2016

Inter urinas et faeces nascimur (We are born between urine and excrement) — Saint Augustine

If there's one theme that's sure to raise a laugh among children, it's poo. Indeed, anything that enters the somatic or semantic halo of excrement is good to go. Take the Australian children's author Andy Griffiths, who's made a genuine fortune from his book *The Day My Bum Went Psycho* and its sequels, including *Zombie Bums from Uranus* and *Bumageddon*. The plot summary is illuminating: one night Zack Freeman follows his self-detaching bum to a secret meeting, where he learns of a conspiracy of bums who are plotting to take over the world by creating a gigantic fart; when this uber-fart has rendered all humans unconscious, the bums will sit in the place of the heads of their old masters. Griffiths's carnivalesque talents for literally turning shit into gold – or, at least, the allegorical image of shit into gold – stands as a kind of emblem of the endlessly fascinating powers of poo for humans in general.

Of course, indecently protracted poo-bum jokes and expressions are undeniably as good for adults as they are for children: think of the common slang phrases shit so successfully supports. *She's a shit-stirrer, he's a shit-eater, I'm shit-scared, you're shitting me, they're shit-kickers*, and so on, are only a few of the many idiomatic expressions celebrating this ambivalent substance, not to mention the perennial appeal of fart gags, toilet humour and whoopee cushions.

And the appeal of shit is not just reserved for children or slang: the Belgian artist Wim Delvoye's notorious *Cloaca* series, for example, comprises impressive chemico-mechanical contraptions that mimic the mammalian digestive system. In a strangely satisfying spectacle, viewers can watch the gleaming glass-and-steel machine being fed 'real food' amidst the choking methane stench of 'real shit'. The *Cloaca* series in some ways functions as a microcosm for art in general: it exposes the disavowed bond between excrement and civilisation, between life and technology, in a fashion that is at once mildly humorous and slightly repulsive. The contraption strikes just the right balance of idealisation and perversion: art is what you get when you mix high with low, raising up waste as if it were a special treasure. The sublimating alchemy of high art shows how it's the lowest functions that bring us together.

Yet this still doesn't quite answer the question: why are there so many jokes, turns of phrase, and general levity across almost all known cultures when the fundamental issue of poo is raised? Why is shit so powerful? And why is it so funny? Why is it so powerful and funny at the same time?

Fart Sound Alarm Clock

Aside from artists, agricultural industries, and waste-management enterprises, psychoanalysis has taken more than a professional interest in the project. If Sigmund Freud remains known for allegedly making every elongated object a phallic symbol – 'sometimes a cigar's just a cigar,' that is, the rest of the time a smoker's really chomping on dicks – as well as for his theories of sexual repression, we shouldn't forget that his analyses place poo at the throbbing centre of human life (I've heard so many awful jokes about the *anal* in *analytic*, it's hard to retain my excitement for the pun, but let's not deny that it's there).

Freud's masterpiece *The Interpretation of Dreams* (1900) is full of shit, without any exaggeration, and without any prejudice. As Freud emphasised: What is it that all of us do, that we clearly make ourselves, and yet so often seems foreign to ourselves? We excrete and we dream. Dreams sizzle with images of obscenity accompanied by extreme affects of excitement, shame, anger, anxiety and terror. Teeth leak from mouths, students walk about pantless, patients fail to be able to have dinner parties. But there's also an inordinate amount of shit about. Freud packs the tract with his own exemplary dreams, one of which runs as follows:

Richard Newton, *Treason!!!*, 1798, satirical etching

It is a short dream, which will fill every reader with disgust. A hill, on which there was something like an open-air closet: a very long seat with a large hole at the end of it. Its back edge was thickly covered with small heaps of faeces of all sizes and degrees of freshness. There were bushes behind the seat. I micturated on the seat; a long stream of urine washed everything clean; the lumps of faeces came away easily and fell into the opening. It was as though at the end there was still some left. Why did I feel no disgust during this dream?

Note that Freud expressly frames the account in terms of *disgust*. From the moment we are born, we are taught to feel disgust for our shit. The anus is private, perhaps the most private of all our orifices: closed even when open. You need to be taught this to live in society, to keep your anus and its products hidden.

If, in Freud's account, the reader will be disgusted, Freud makes it clear that Freud-the-dreamer was not: the lack of such an affect in the face of excremental obscenity is therefore a noteworthy feature of the dream itself. Freud establishes the deep complicity of the unconscious with shit by pointing to the recurrence of the latter throughout literary history. In his discussion, he happily draws on, among other things, Greek myth (the Labours of Hercules), Jonathan Swift's *Gulliver's Travels*, and Rabelais's *Gargantua and Pantagruel*, as well as sundry quotidian details regarding contemporaneous Italian water closets and historical facts about Notre Dame of Paris.

From the moment we are born, we are taught to feel disgust for our shit.

Freud's dream turns out to validate his own theories of dreaming: wish-fulfillment. This is a dream of power, and who better to blow away the shit – like God supposedly blew the Spanish Armada away from England – than Freud himself? That shit functions as a paradigmatic image of power comes as no surprise. Shitting is always political, at least for human beings. Here's this thing that comes from the inside of your body, that isn't your body, that can't stay part of your body, and which you can't properly live with when it's outside your body. Something has to be done to it; you can't just leave it alone or let it be. You must not wallow in your shit; shit has to be monitored, treated, spirited away.

★★★

In his *Three Essays on the Theory of Sexuality* (1905), Freud asserts:

> The characteristics of infantile sexual life which we have hitherto emphasized are the facts that it is essentially auto-erotic (i.e. that it finds its object in the infant's own body) and that its individual component instincts are upon the whole disconnected and independent of one another in their search for pleasure.

According to Freud, infants experience a disorderly bundle of obscure drives that cause them to seek satisfaction wherever they can find it. This gives Freud the impetus to drill a little further down into the archaeology of excrement. What are the three most important orifices in the relation between a child and its parents or caretakers? The mouth, the anus, the genitals.

These correspond to Freud's notorious three phases of development, the oral, the anal, and the genital. The infant's first concern is oral: sucking and screaming, gulping in air and milk, belching out a virtuoso range of noises according to its scrambled affects. But where there's ingestion, there's excretion. Not that the kid might care about this for some time, but the parents certainly do. Shit is the first gift of the child to its parents: *Here's something I made that I want you to have.* It's a metamorphic and self-dissimulating treat, a product that the child can work with, if not always altogether control. But it's also the object of strenuous attention from the parents: *Don't do it here, do it there! Don't do it now, do it then! Don't talk about it, just do it properly*!

Shit is at once one of the most precious of substances, yet the one struck with the most restrictive prohibitions. The anal phase is a key moment for Freud in the development of the super-ego, that minatory internal agency that functions as an inexhaustible resource of guilt at the very heart of the psyche. Yet for that very reason, it's also very strongly cathected, that is, invested with all sorts of exciting-if-disavowed intensities. It's no wonder that, with this horrible mixture of excitement, abjection, guilt, and so on, that an entire unconscious complex should literally come to be built on top of and out of this shit. From then on, concealed avatars of excrement turn up in all sorts of unexpected places. One example: given children's lack of sexual knowledge, or, rather, their capacity to doubt any information regarding procreation that their parents see fit to deliver them, it's no wonder that infantile theories regarding the origin of babies are legion. Freud relates the disturbingly common spontaneity of the 'cloacal theory' among children, which is that babies are shat out from the anus...

He-Gassen (Fart Competitions), a Japanese art scroll created during
the Edo period (1603–1868) by an unknown artist or artists

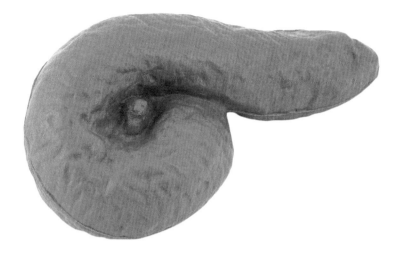

Fake poo

The fundamental role played by this poo-complex in human psychic development helps to explain its abiding role in universal humour. In his own little treatise on the subject, *Jokes and their Relation to the Unconscious* (1905), Freud comments that humour is the correlate of a 'lifting of repression'. Yet a lifting of repression is not tantamount to understanding; on the contrary, for Freud, *we laugh without understanding why it is we laugh*. The quasi-transgressive fun of poo is a defence against the threat to our psychology raised by this brown spectre, the repression of which we will continue to ensure – exactly at the moment that we give ourselves the false alibi of acknowledging it by laughing. Our relation to shit is necessarily physically, psychologically, and socially repressed, so any attempt to speak of it sensibly is going to come a cropper; it is, nevertheless, close to being a genuine universal, being shared by children and adults, men and women, ancient and contemporary cultures. This is why Freud can write:

> The sexual material which forms the content of smut includes more than what is *peculiar* to each sex; it also includes what is *common* to both sexes and to which the feeling of shame extends – that is to say, what is excremental in the most comprehensive sense. This is, however, the sense covered by sexuality in childhood, an age at which there is, as it were, a cloaca within which what is sexual and what is excremental are barely or not at all distinguished. Throughout the whole range of the psychology of the neuroses, what is sexual includes what is excremental, and is understood in the old, infantile, sense.

Extraordinary and far-reaching as such a claim may be –
that humans will never be able to quite remove the shit from
sexuality, nor the fun from farting – it's not Freud's final word
on the subject.

In what is perhaps one of the craziest footnotes ever penned,
Freud speculates in *Civilization and its Discontents* (1930):

> The diminution of the olfactory stimuli seems itself to
> be a consequence of man's raising himself from the ground,
> of his assumption of an upright gait; this made his genitals,
> which were previously concealed, visible and in need
> of protection, and so provoked feelings of shame in him.
> The fateful process of civilization would thus have set in
> with man's adoption of an erect posture.

Let's take a moment to appreciate the visionary lunacy of
this assertion: *The development of the human species is itself the
consequence of an organic repression of the smell of shit.*

A four-legged creature, the human ancestor, is running
along the ground, its nose close to the earth where smells cling
and linger; suddenly, it smells something truly revolting, and rears
up and back in disgust; if it makes a habit of this becoming-erect,
its nose is literally raised in the air where the trace of the scents
are confused in the breezes; as a result, its eyes start to become more useful to it than its nose, and, as they begin to bulge more prominently, the muzzle concomitantly begins to retreat

When we snigger at shit we are sniggering at the determining cause of our own evolution

into the head, freeing the mouth to make articulate sounds;
moreover, the forelegs are freed to become arms with grasping
hands. Yet this new posture also exposes the genitals to vision:
the becoming-erect of humanity installs a feeling of shame at the
very origin of the species.

On this description, when we snigger at shit we are
sniggering at the determining cause of our own evolution.
No wonder our bums are plotting to go psycho.

Engineer
Sian Thomas

'People sometimes refer to the tunnels as a cathedral of sewage.'

What do you do?
I'm an engineer by training and I've spent a lot of my career working in sewage. I got involved in the construction of a new sewage treatment works in Reading and then operated a number of treatment plants at Thames Water. Now I'm working on the Thames Tideway Tunnel, London's new sewer.

Did you anticipate a career in sewage?
My father was a mechanical engineer so I grew up encouraged to learn about the infrastructures that support our world. We flush the chain and we're not interested in what happens after – but this is critical infrastructure.

How does our current sewerage system work?
We're still using Joseph Bazalgette's system. As London developed, the rivers were built over and became sewers. In the 1850s there came a point where there was so much sewage and rubbish in the River Thames that Bazalgette was commissioned to do something about

it. He collected sewage flow that would otherwise have gone into the Thames and took it from west London to east London, to two outfall sites. Here the sewage was held before being released into the outgoing tide.

Has the system changed much since?
Over time Thames Water constructed treatment plants at these sites, but otherwise not much. There were only a couple of million people in London when he built the system, and he designed it for four million – now there are about eight million people that rely on it. He was really forward thinking.

So why the need for this new super sewer?
Bazalgette built an overflow into the system, so that when it rained, sewage would overflow into the river. Today, because there are more people, we have a lot of concrete and rainfall patterns are different, there's more run-off. As little as two millimetres of rainfall in London fills the sewerage system to capacity.

How often does this happen?
On average, in a year, it's the equivalent of almost once a week.

Where will the new sewer run?
It will run at a downward gradient from west to east London, roughly underneath the Thames – and underneath everything else – and connect to the pre-existing Lee Tunnel.

How are you going to build it?
We'll excavate a series of large round shafts at three locations across London. From these shafts, tunnelling machines will be lowered into the ground – these are huge seven-metre-diameter drilling heads that eat their way through the ground. Behind the drilling head is a whole production line: concrete segments get slotted into place and then as the machine moves forward the material that is excavated gets taken out.

What will happen to overflow once the new sewer is built?
The new sewer creates a diversion route for it. The overflow is lowered into the tunnel using vortex generators. These force the sewage to spin round in circles so that it drops in a controlled fashion to the bottom of the shaft – up to 65 metres below ground – without damaging the tunnel.

Do you have to hack into the existing tunnels at any point?
Yeah, there's a complex network of pipes underground, so we work with Thames Water to find out where we need to make those connections and then divert the sewage while we're joining them.

What's it like down there?
People sometimes refer to the tunnels as a cathedral of sewage – there's some amazing brickwork. It's a real privilege to stand in one of them. It's interesting to see what really happens underground.

Are you very aware that you are in a sewer?
Yes, absolutely. In order to go into a sewer, you need to be prepped. You need the right clothes and we have to take gas monitors so that we can monitor the gasses for safety. It's a very controlled operation.

People have complained that Tideway is a 'nineteenth-century approach to a twenty-first century problem,' do they have a point?
If you're starting from scratch then you can do all kinds of things, but the system as it exists…some of those early decisions defined what the system would be. In London, we have a combined sewerage system; the dirty water from toilets and the surface water get mixed in the same pipes. In new builds they're separated, so you can do much more in terms of sustainable drainage, and making interventions in the landscape to mitigate the amount of run-off.

If you could start from scratch, then, what model of toilet would you suggest?
In rural areas you can be much smarter; many people in the UK have their own cesspits close to their homes. You can manage that when you have a low density of people. But as soon as you get lots of people in the same place, you simply need proper infrastructure to deal with the problem.

The Quilton baby

The Soft Sell

When it comes to marketing toilet paper, cuteness is key. Design critic *Alice Twemlow* takes a swipe at all those cupids, puppies and fluffy clouds.

'Our brand of toilet paper is the softest,' each pastel-hued heat-printed package cajoles us:

> See how this baby duck has chosen to nest among our absorbent, aloe-infused multi-ply sheets, or how that koala cub hugs our huggable roll instead of its mother, and observe this little puppy having the time of its life unravelling our quilted roll around the house.

The hope is that these images will befuddle us sufficiently to prevent us from considering the lack of any real technological innovation in toilet paper over the past 120 years, and to postpone any self-reflection on what we are actually doing with it, which is far from nesting in it, seeking emotional comfort in its embrace, or, unfurling it along the corridor, but rather using it to wipe away excess urine and faeces from our perineal and anal regions.

Anthropologist Mary Douglas writes, 'Reflection on dirt involves reflection on the relation of order to disorder, being to non-being, form to formlessness, life to death.' Toilet paper, just one of the many products we use to erase or disguise the smell, sight and touch of excremental dirt, contrives – through the design of its packaging – to distract us from any such reflection. The packages conjure purifying imagery, ranging from the celestial to the cute, in order to imaginatively transport us away from the facts of our daily deposits of water, inorganic salts, hormones, metabolites, bacterial biomass, protein, carbohydrate, undigested plant matter, fat, calcium and iron phosphates, intestinal secretions, dried epithelial cells, and mucus. Blue cumulus cloud-strewn skies elevate us from the baseness of our digestive tracts and from the bowels of the earth where sewers are. Kittens, puppies and bear cubs take us back in time, away from the adult responsibilities of personal hygiene and thoughts of death, to the innocent freedom of pre-sphincter-control infancy.

Once here, of course, it's hard to avoid Freud. According to his psychosexual development theory, between the ages of around eighteen months and three years (the time of toilet training) the human infant's libido is concentrated in the erogenous zone of the anus. For the child, the anal product becomes symbolic and may be used for play, as a gift, a weapon or as property. When this anal stage comes to an end, so Freud's theory goes, the symbolism originally attached to the anal product gets attached to other non-bodily objects, and ultimately continues repressed in the subconscious. Indeed, the connection between anal retentiveness and a preoccupation with property ownership, for example, recalls the phenomenon of hoarding, illustrated most dramatically (and appropriately in this instance) on episodes of cable network TLC's reality television show *Extreme Couponing*, where people stockpile up to forty years worth of toilet paper in their closets.

The toilet product industry takes the two-ply social pressure of hygiene and convention and packages it into new, multi-billion-dollar-generating combinations, the latest of which is the moist toilet tissue. Wipes, made of long synthetic or cotton fibres moistened with water or other liquids like isopropyl alcohol, and lotion, were invented in the late 1950s, became a common means of dealing with dirty babies' bottoms by the early 1990s and then began gaining popularity as a product for all the family and not just babies around 2010. The most extreme efforts to rebrand the product are in the male market group, perhaps because of an enduring physical issue noted in 1564 by satirist Francois Rabelais that 'Who his foul tail with paper wipes, Shall at his ballocks leave some chips.'

Among the many new male-oriented products are One-Wipe-Charlies – peppermint-scented, packaged in a metallic-coloured plastic pouch, and, according to one of the product's 1,870 reviews, are 'like wiping your fanny with silk, but far less messy,' – and Dude Wipes, which are encased in black condom-wrapper-like packages, with an industrial-techno logo. The straightforward and irreverent tone of their advertising targets frat boys interested in salvaging what the Dude Wipes founders call 'stanky' situations.

Unfortunately, the growing use of wipes is creating its own 'stanky' situation. Most wipes have long synthetic fibres that, once flushed, do not break down in water and accumulate problematically in our sewerage systems creating what *The New York Times* graphically referred to as 'dank clusters'. In 2013 the world's largest recorded 'fatberg' – a grotesque-sounding ten-tonne, bus-sized lump of fat and so-called 'flushable' wipes – was found in a London sewer and took three weeks to be dismantled.

As toilet roll sales in the West begin to plateau, their manufacturers are finding ways to sell both toilet paper and toilet tissue wipes as a two-step process. In 2012 Kimberly-Clark began encouraging consumers to use the company's dry and moist toilet paper products in combination (and to come up with a term – such as 'Southern Hospitality' and 'Clean Getaway' – for doing so). Currently they are advocating the process through a #GoCommando campaign targeting summer festival-goers, who have the opportunity, thanks to Cottonelle, to 'achieve a higher state of confidence'.

Similarly, British firm Andrex, which launched moist toilet tissues as early as 1992, is now marketing what they call the Andrex Clean Routine to parents and kids using endorsements by psychologists and downloadable star charts. The Clean Routine recommends the use of three to four sheets of toilet paper per wipe, followed by the application of one to two sheets of moist toilet tissue, and a final patting dry with another wad of toilet roll. Any household with small children will surely find this added five-step routine to be an extra and unnecessary social pressure, and ultimately more cumbersome than relieving.

As literary theorist and sociologist Roland Barthes observed of 1950s French commercial culture, manufacturers of cleaning products need to plant the idea of dirtiness as a social evil in order that they can sell the remedy. In his article 'Sapanoids and Detergents', he identified differences in the marketing of various soap powders and detergents. Some, like Persil, based their marketing on the evidence of a *result*: the presentation of a piece of laundry which is 'whiter', and therefore superior, appealed to vanity and social prestige. Others, like Omo, emphasised the *process* of cleaning: they attempted to engage the consumer in what Barthes described as 'a sort of experiential mode of substance', implicating him/her as 'the accomplice of deliverance'. Today's toilet products show the same variations in marketing. When buying toilet tissue we are presented with the idea that its application will result in our anus being rendered as clean as a newborn koala's; the imagery used to sell toilet cleaner,

When buying toilet tissue we are presented with the idea that its application will result in our anus being rendered as clean as a newborn koala's

however, invites the consumer to participate in the cleaning process via depictions of magic wands, sudsy bubbles, and gels, which produce such dazzlingly blue, light-suffused sparkling vortexes of cleanliness we are almost tempted to dive in after them.

The softness-, cleanliness-evoking toilet roll brand names such as Purex, Cushelle, Velvet, White Cloud and Quilted Northern, are rendered on their packaging, unsurprisingly, in white, puffy flowing type. The backgrounds tend to be gradated pastel-hued floral hazes, the visual equivalent of generic elevator Muzak. There is a preponderance of swirls, stylised banners, festoons, curves and swooshes evoking a stream of toilet paper flowing in the wind, one supposes, as well as the ensuing imagined caress of the tissue on one's skin, or the hoped-for smoothness of one's evacuation.

The Cushelle koala

But these graphics also continue a trend observed by design historians Abbott Miller and Ellen Lupton in their seminal book on the evolution of American kitchen and bathroom design between 1890 and 1940, *The Bathroom, the Kitchen and the Aesthetics of Waste* (1997), which is that 'the aesthetics of waste is streamlined'. The metaphor of streamlining invokes a body moving efficiently through fluid; but it can also refer to the acceleration of the cycle of purchase and disposal so essential to modern capitalist economics. Lupton and Miller write, 'The policy of "planned obsolescence" pictured the economy itself as a "body" whose health depends on a continual cycle of production and waste, ingestion and excretion.' Advertising provides a vital and 'lubricating' role (as Lupton and Miller aptly put it) in hastening that cycle of mass distribution, a 'laxative for hastening the flow of goods through the economy.'

Toilet paper, like a tissue or sanitary pad, is the poster child for disposable mass culture. Utterly expendable, its sole function is to be used up and discarded. It is a 'physical and symbolic' consumable, as design critic Reyner Banham put it in 1963, referring to the list of items the character Lolita gathers to soothe and normalise her disturbing way of life, and that Vladimir Nabakov uses to stand in for mass-produced American modernity in his novel: 'In the gay town of Lepingville I bought her four books of comics, a box of candy, a box of sanitary pads, two cokes, a manicure set...a portable radio, chewing gum...' Yet paper was used for anal and perineal cleansing many hundreds of years prior to industrialised mass production, in early medieval China. The scholar-official Yan Zhitui acknowledged both the practice and his respect for literature in 589 AD, when he wrote, 'Paper on which there are quotations or commentaries from the Five Classics or the names of sages, I dare not use for toilet purposes.'

Rural Americans in the 1800s seem to have had a similarly refined view of what made toilet-appropriate paper. Before the widespread marketing of paper tissue specifically for use in the toilet, many families used pages torn from the Sears and Roebuck mail-order catalogue in their outhouses. Some catalogues even had a hole in the corner so they could be hung on a nail near the toilet. The use of the catalogue declined in the 1930s when Sears began printing on glossy, clay-coated paper, which made it less absorbent.

In the UK too, toilet paper's heritage is linked to advertising. In her memoir of a 1920s childhood, Diana Holman-Hunt recalls being asked by her grandmother to cut a stack of 'circulars, envelopes and paper bags' into squares for use in the toilet. She writes:

> When I had cut a hundred sheets, I pierced their corners and threaded them with a string; I tied this in a loop to hang on a nail by the "convenience." I made a mental note of the softer pieces and put them together in the middle, between the back of a calendar from Barkers and an advertisement for night-lights.

While early flush toilets, increasingly common in wealthy American homes by the 1860s, were disguised and enclosed with cabinetry and built to resemble chairs, early mass-produced toilet paper was presented more explicitly. Gayetty's Medicated Paper for the Water Closet, patented in 1857, was folded into sheets and sold in red-printed paper packages, and advertised in a *New York Daily Tribune* advertisement as 'the greatest discovery of modern times so far as alleviating and preventing human suffering is concerned.' One can see a return to this Victorian apothecary aesthetic in the use of a hyperbolic verbal rhetoric, blocky letterpress and woodcuts, and type-only packaging designs in products aimed at the bearded hipster market, such as Dr. Bronner's Castile Soap products, Aesop-APC deodorising poo drops, and the Victorianesque fly transfer put in Schipol airport urinals to increase better aiming and to reduce cleaning costs.

For, today, while those pastel petals and puppies still dominate the middle-market, there are distinct variations at either end of the toilet-roll and toilet-cleaning product spectrum: at the low end, value and bulk-buy brands are almost wilfully basic, with one-colour printing, bold sans serif typefaces, and nary a kitten nor a waterfall in sight; at the luxury end, indeed somewhere beyond it, you'll find Joseph's Toiletries, which sell for sixty euros per box of ribbon-tied, specially woven and vitamin-coated toilet tissues made of one hundred percent tender virgin new-growth cellulose fibres, and which promises 'profound softness', when paired with a Gentle Cleanser made with Swiss glacier water and a Balancing Care moisturiser. This extravagant product assemblage is styled with quiet luxurious conservatism in gold and white, with centred serif type.

So what is it with all these bowers of fluffy clouds and equally fluffy baby animals? What is it with all this softness? It's not biologically necessary; we used to use corn cobs, moss and stones, and in many countries a jug of water and the left hand suffice, and are considered far superior to smearing the dirt around with paper. But the hyperbolic softness does seem to be psychologically desirable. Global personal care brands have established toilet paper and its ilk as flattering to what Barthes characterised as 'those obscure impulses of caressing envelopment.' It has transmogrified from its origins as wood shavings (indeed, early users often complained of finding splinters) and now makes us think of clouds, duckling down, cotton balls, and babies' bottoms. The Charmin tagline introduced in 1956, 'Charmin babies your skin', seems, in retrospect to have signalled the current tendencies of toilet product packaging toward encouraging our infantile regressive impulses for comfort that we seek both in our hard, industrialised, and enamelled bathrooms, and in our hard, adult world.

The Charmin bears

Two gay men dressed as women pee against a wall during the Belgian Pride Parade, 2013

A Piss-Poor Performance

What does it take to design a truly gender-neutral toilet? With debates raging across the US, artist *Alex Schweder* stands up for women who do the same.

Let's begin with married couple Heike and Bill (not their real names) who are German and American respectively. German men, according to Heike, are less concerned than their American counterparts about acting out a masculine persona at home. Bill, however, associates feeling free to do what he wants in the bathroom with a sense of being at home; he likes standing up at the toilet to pee. This disgusts Heike. She says that every time she hears Bill using the toilet in this way, she has the image of herself down on her knees cleaning up his piss; this is not the kind of woman she is or wants to be. Bill defends himself by pointing out that he cleans the bathroom often. The tension between them mounts and she tersely retorts that while he maybe cleans the bathroom once a week, he splashes the toilet with his urine several times a day. The question arises as to why Bill doesn't just sit down to urinate, to which he answers that he feels like a sissy doing that, and with all the nagging by Heike, he would feel 'pussy whipped' were he to give in to what he saw as her demands. With the emotional temperature rising, Heike replies that his feeling like a sissy while sitting to pee is ridiculous. 'That is silly, I don't feel like a man when I pee standing in the shower!' she snaps. Bill's face turns ashen; he had no idea that Heike peed in the shower. 'I don't pee in the shower. That's disgusting,' he says. 'You get up earlier than I do which means that I stand in your piss when I shower after you.' 'Well that's how I feel when I use your splashed-on toilet,' she rebukes, 'and besides, the shower water cleans it all away, which is more than you do.'

Seven years ago I began an architectural practice whereby I renovate people's homes by changing the ways they use, discuss, and think about them rather than through any material change.

As part of this practice, I meet with people in my studio for an hour-long conversation about their homes. The success of this discursive branch of what I call performance architecture has led me to establish SOAP (Schweder's Office for Architectural Performances). The above exchange occurred when Heike and Bill came to me with a specific renovation in mind. From the altercation, it is clear that the toilet – and the way men and women use it – is a flashpoint and site of struggle for both our gender identity and also the way women and men relate to one another.

Human beings have designed this thing – the toilet – a place where our corporeal interior is externalised, where our bodies become not our bodies. Yet at or on the toilet we are more than just animals that stand or sit.

Of course, whether we choose to stand or sit is not engrained but learned. 'One is not born, but rather becomes, a woman,' Simone de Beauvoir famously declared in *The Second Sex* (1973). The psychoanalyst Jacques Lacan also saw gender differences as illusory. For him, the segregation of men's and women's restrooms are the culmination of 'laws of urinary segregation'; these are enforced when little children are toilet-trained, when boys and girls are taught to adopt specific postures in order to pee.

Anxieties about gender lie just below the bathroom's glossy white surface

Design also figures in the performance of gender, and public restrooms perhaps provide the clearest example of how gender identity is constructed through design. In their introduction to the book *Ladies and Gents: Public Toilets and Gender* (2009), Olga Gershenson and Barbara Penner write, 'Public toilets are among the last openly sex-segregated spaces that remain in our society and, crucially, among the last spaces that people *expect* to be sex-segregated.' Conventional segregated bathrooms draw clear lines. Not only do they separate men and women from one another, but also men from men and women from women. Toilet and urinal partitions prevent bodily mingling of same sex occupants through either gaze or touch. Sound and smell are permeable but these unpleasant emissions might further serve to stop bodies gravitating towards one another. Conventional restrooms are theatres in which binary gender identities are performed, witnessed and reinforced. By passing through gendered doors we choose which role we will play.

Students stage a 'shit-in' protest in 2015 at Simon Fraser University, Burnaby, Canada to advocate for gender-inclusive bathrooms.

You only need to mark what happens when a man walks into the ladies' or a woman into the men's to know that objections arise when people choose the 'wrong' door; anxieties about gender lie just below the bathroom's glossy white surface. That any transgression of this binary equation – that man equals male and woman equals female – creates social anxieties is evidenced by events in the USA this year. In March 2016, North Carolina became the first US state to pass a law, the Public Facilities Privacy and Security Act (or 'bathroom bill' as it's come to be known), requiring that transgender people use only bathrooms that match their biological – rather than identified – gender. Several other states considered similar action, including Illinois, Kansas, Massachusetts, Missouri, Mississippi, South Dakota and Tennessee. In May, the Obama administration issued a directive to all schools receiving federal funds, that they must protect the freedom of students to choose which bathroom to use regardless of their sex or gender identity. Eleven state-filed lawsuits contesting this executive advocacy shortly followed. 'Shit-in' protests demanding gender-neutral toilets followed at various universities – but they didn't have the desired effect. In August, Texas and another twelve states asked a federal judge to halt the Obama administration's directive.

On one level there is little architectural difference between the ladies' and gents' rooms: their finishes are the same, the toilets themselves are identical, and both sexes go in for the same reason. The most pronounced distinction between the two spaces is the addition of the urinal. This tangible addition prescribes a specific posture so that through it we have come to associate peeing upright with the enactment of masculinity while thinking of seated relief as feminine. For de Beauvoir this very process marks the decline into sexual oppression, when girls are taught to crouch in a subordinate position while boys are encouraged to stand proud and produce the perfect arc.

Philosopher Judith Butler, whose seminal contribution to gender theory is her concept of 'performativity', insists that people's agency in their own gender comes when they change the way that they perform it. They can do this by subverting the norms of the society into which they are born. A good example of this is the transgender person passing through a bathroom door.

For the man or woman who identifies with the opposite gender from which their biology is usually associated – or with both the choice of toilet door represents a calibration of priorities: should they, when going to the bathroom, privilege their biology or their gender identity? The preference for standing or sitting could also be important to their sense of gender identity and its enactment. The choice of toilet door then – and whether one chooses to stand or sit – can be a complex issue.

Given this, perhaps the key to a truly gender-neutral toilet – and to its widespread acceptance – will involve a thorough reconsideration of how we all *use* the toilet. If we become more aware of design's complicity in the performance of certain gender roles and social mores – urinals, toilets, and in fact the whole of our bathroom environment are props that assist us in this performance – how could design make space for or entertain the possibility of other performances? Sometimes this could involve changing the object and sometimes it could involve changing the story around the object, as will be the case when we return to Heike and Bill.

Many who advocate for men's seated evacuation, for example, cite health benefits, cleanliness, etiquette and empathy towards their female counterparts as reasons. However, none of these are at the heart of the matter and to shift male behaviour from standing to sitting, the performance of masculinity is what needs to be addressed. Similarly, to shift female behaviour from sitting to standing, the performance of femininity needs to be addressed. Towards this, there are three strategies that can be pursued: make it possible for women to perform femininity

 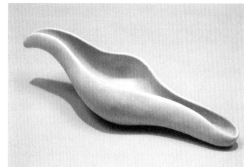

 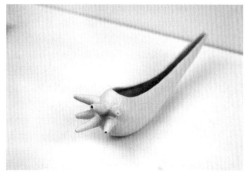

Kim Dickey, *Lady J Series*, 1994–1999

standing, design the urinal in such a way that it becomes problematic to perform a macho persona, and make sitting on the toilet to pee more masculine than standing.

The belief that only men can stand and pee is supported by over a century of public practice. Between 1994 and 1999, however, ceramic artist Kim Dickey challenged this presumption by developing a vitreous china prosthetic that allows women to urinate while erect. Made from the same material as the toilet itself, her *Lady J Series* takes its name from another plastic device advertised for use when camping. Dickey's small china spout is held between a woman's legs and directs her urine as a penis would. Unlike the pure functionalism of the original Lady J – or of the cardboard P-Mate distributed to women at Glastonbury Festival in 2004 – Dickey's recasting of this object introduced play, pleasure, humour and theatre to the act of peeing. She referenced a number of gendered and non-gendered forms such as uncircumcised penises, breasts, codpieces, Renaissance multi-spout fountains, watering cans, and bear claws in her designs.

In contrast, architect Yolande Daniels addressed the design of the urinal itself and its entrenched association with masculinity, in her work. Her *FEMMEpissoire* (1996) augmented the urinal with typically feminine accoutrements while also enabling a woman to pee in a different posture. While female urinals were put into production half a century earlier, Daniels's was the first female urinal to allow its user to observe her body evacuating itself of urine. Daniels achieved this by attaching stirrups to the sides of the pissoire, which cup and support the user's upper legs (the stirrups also reference the hygienic familiarity of a doctor's office). Rather than squatting, the stirrups enable a woman to lean back, face forward, and project her pee. Daniels addressed the practical concern of soiled clothing by also designing special pants with a zipper that reveals the entirety of a woman's crotch. She also placed a mirror above the toilet bowl at face height with a lipstick holder at its base. The convergence of the urinal with these conventionally feminine accoutrements cues a hybrid performance, both masculine and feminine. If, as is suggested by Daniels's design, women en mass begin using urinals and the urinal becomes, like the toilet, a post-gender or gender-neutral object, then perhaps in the future the urinal will be able to shed these feminising limbs. The hope is that serial enactment could lead to a new normal.

While the previous two works imposed feminine performance onto masculine practices, another strategy is to multiply the masculinities invested in an object by queering the urinal. Inspired by both Daniels and Dickey, in 2001 I undertook a residency at the ceramics factory of the Kohler sanitary-ware company in Sheboygan, Wisconsin. I used my time at Kohler to produce the *Bi-Bardon* urinal, a plumbing fixture named after the Kohler product line from which this conjoined urinal was made. The birth defect of disambiguation that this urinal references invites a defiance of the conventional bathroom etiquette associated with urinals; that is, to ignore your neighbour. Partitions between urinals consolidate this behaviour, but the fixture I designed places the men using it much closer to one another. Here they enact conjoined twins, see one another's genitals and have to confront any perceived or real attraction to one another. The conjoined urinal suggests a different kind of masculinity – not the kind most men are comfortable with – from that which is normalised by most bathroom design.

While fully functional, all three of these speculative alternative gender performances involving the toilet only exist in the space of the exhibition. Any of them could be put into production were there popular desire for them. But in truth, the clamour for objects that prompt other performances of gender is not coming from the mainstream, but from queer minorities. Bringing a product to market is expensive and time-consuming with no guarantee of success, which is why I put forward a third way of recasting gender enactment in relation to the toilet: changing the stories about who we are in relation to them.

This strategy for multiplying the possible performances of gender in the bathroom requires reshaping the perspective we often have of men who sit to pee from emasculating to

Ronit Eisenbach, *Installations by Architects: Experiments in
Building and Design*, Princeton Architectural Press, 2009.

Yolande Daniels, *FEMMEpissoire*, 1996

Alex Schweder, *Bi-Bardon Urinal*, 2001

Earlier this year the cast of Broadway musical *Kinky Boots* released
a song, *Just Pee* in support of transgender bathroom rights.

empowering. Let's return then to Heike and Bill, who we left
entrenched and angry over the splashing of urine in both the
shower and on the toilet seat. An analysis of their exchange reveals
that what each wanted had less to do with an idea of gender than
it did with control. Bill felt his power compromised – for many
men power is associated with masculinity, making it hard to
disentangle the two – if he let Heike control him through how he
pees. Heike on the other hand felt coerced into the performance
of a femininity she did not like. Their architectural renovation
was to give them each a say in how the other used the bathroom
to pee. Both expressed disgust at the perceived filth of the
other, and both could influence the other by changing the ways
they themselves behaved. In the end, both dropped their guns
simultaneously: each agreed to stop peeing standing up when at
home. For that we should give them both a seated ovation.

Paleoscatologist
Andrew Jones

'One type was known to emerge from every orifice of the human body including the nose and the corner of the eye.'

What is a paleoscatologist?
A paleoscatologist looks at old excrement, ancient coprolite – or fossilised faeces – dung and faecal matter.

How did you become a paleoscatologist?
I went to college and studied zoology, and when I had to elect a special subject, I chose parasites. One of the main things you look at in parasitology is faecal samples; I got involved with archaeological work and found that a lot of faecal materials were excavated on digs.

What can faecal matter tell you archaeologically that other artefacts can't?
They tell us about the health of organisms. From them you can get some insight into local hygiene practices, sanitation and the ways that people dealt with filth and rubbish generally. It adds to the picture of what life was really like for people in different places and times

in the past, rather than just observing the size of their houses or what building materials they used.

Tell us about the Lloyds Bank Turd you are famous for.
I was working in East Angola in the early 1970s and heard rumours about a coprolite from the Viking age in York. When I went there and asked about it, everyone thought it was lost. But we found it in a wooden tobacco box. It resembled a piece of human faeces but it was very hard, so we couldn't be certain. When we examined it microscopically, we found a very large number of human parasitic nematode worm eggs, which showed that it was both faecal and human.

How big is it?
It is nineteen and a half centimetres long.

Do you think it was just this Viking who had worms?
No, we've also looked at a whole range of rubbish pits and latrine pits, which

show how endemic parasites were to Viking cities. It would be fair to say that it was normal to be parasitised in Viking-age York and possibly throughout the medieval period, to be frank. People were living in very close proximity and they didn't have a faeces disposal system that physically separated them from their excrement, so the chance of re-infection was very high.

What was life like living with worms?
People can live pretty full, active lives with worms. Worms would have been encountered when taking out the chamber pot. They were a feature of life whereas today they are extremely rare. One type was known to emerge from every orifice of the human body including the nose and the corner of the eye. You don't hear these stories any longer. I sometimes think, if you look at the Viking mythology of dragons – at all their interlacing patterns and decorations which often had animal forms that were very elongated and winding – perhaps they saw 'worminess' as reflected in their mythological beliefs. The Vikings believed there was some great big snake-like, worm-like thing surrounding the whole of the ocean. They believed in a flat world, not in a globe or sphere.

What other interesting discoveries have you made?
I got involved in a project looking at some posh houses in Pompeii. They were excavated about two hundred years ago. We found that the internal drainage systems in several of these houses hadn't really been properly recorded or analysed, and we managed to find deposits in tube systems. These were ceramic pipes built into walls that carried waste. We found parasite eggs, so these tubes were carrying human excrement among other things. People were just throwing stuff down them and there were no U-bends or anything – no water traps – so flies, rats and vile fumes were coming straight into the buildings. It must have been pretty smelly.

What could you tell about the way these people lived?
There is very good evidence that most of the latrines in domestic houses were located near the kitchen. That's where the slaves worked (the Patrician families didn't do their own cooking). The lavatories were useful for throwing away kitchen waste as well as other sorts of waste and also ashes… Ashes and charcoal would have helped kill off flies and unpleasant noxious fumes.

Can you tell from analysing the poo what the Vikings ate?
A lot of cereal bran, probably wheat or rye. It's likely to have been bread but it could have been some sort of porridge. Also, crushed fragments of fish bone – that tells you a bit about eating habits, that people aren't picking up stuff and putting it on plates; they're crunching up and swallowing things. Eels and herring are abundant. Sometimes leeks and some sort of stone fruit, like a plum.

Why don't you find working with poo unpleasant?
A lot of school kids laugh about it but it's a very good way of engaging with a general audience. Most archaeological finds are difficult to get excited about. If you start talking about lavatories and drains everybody can understand where you're coming from.

Power Toilets

Between 2010 and 2013 art collective *Superflex* erected replicas of the toilets servicing the world's most powerful institutions, in various unlikely locations, for public use. Member *Rasmus Nielsen* explains why.

1

Original
United Nations Security Council,
UN headquarters, New York, USA

Copy
Recreation area, Park van Luna,
Heerhugowaard, The Netherlands, 2010
(designed in collaboration with Nezu Aymo architects)

When we started the *Power Toilet* series, we thought of the
United Nations Security Council toilet, where George W Bush
probably went before he walked into the Security Council and
declared war on Iraq. The security in the building is extreme; you
can't get drawings of it. I would put somebody in jeopardy if I told
you how we got the photos but from them we recreated the toilet.
Now you can use the toilet used by the most powerful people in
the world, and the idea that you are using the toilet that they use
somehow takes away their symbolic power. Why is that? Why does
this reminder that they are part of nature, take something away
from them?

2

Original
JP Morgan Chase executive toilets, JP Morgan
Chase headquarters, New York, USA

Copy
Olympic Restaurant, New York, USA, 2011

The theme of shit and power played out in the context of the 2008
financial crisis. The crisis was hard on Greece and JP Morgan
(who got a US$25 billion bailout) was one of the great sinners.
So we copied the executive toilets from JP Morgan, and put them
in the back of this restaurant, owned by a Greek American.
It got an upgrade, let's put it that way. When you start looking
at numbers, the sort of power these institutions have is absurd.
But I was surprised by how banal JP Morgan's toilets were.
They're into cheap bling; they have much more imagination
when it comes to finance.

3

Original
Ministers' restroom, Justus Lipsius Building,
Council of the European Union, Brussels, Belgium

Copy
Turkish Restaurant Alaturka, Ghent, Belgium, 2012

We're specific about where we put the *Power Toilets*. Turkey
wanted to join the EU, and in 2012 there was a lot of discussion
over whether the Union should invite Turkey to join the party.
So to put these high-level EU toilets in a Turkish context felt a
bit tongue in cheek. Of course the discussion is over now – Turkey
has sided with Russia, it seems – but that's the fate of these toilets;
over time their context can change so much that they change
in meaning.

Photos by Superflex

4

Original
Toilet used by the Executive Board of UNESCO,
UNESCO headquarters, Paris, France

Copy
Guangzhou park, China, 2013
(designed in collaboration with Nezu Aymo architects)

In 1996 we made a biogas system that makes energy out of shit;
it turns shit into power. In a way this cued a deeper understanding
of the weird relationship between power and shit: the power that
you use to fuel a lamp, but also symbolic power. You can use
different kinds of shit to produce energy: cow shit, pig shit and
also human shit. A lot of people don't like this idea even though,
in the amount of energy it can produce, human shit is almost like
uranium. You start on an idea, you do work, and sometimes you
find that there's more to say. You hit on something. It felt like we
weren't done, so to speak.

Photos by Nezu Aymo

Disgraced astronaut Lisa Nowak

Should We All Wear Nappies?

With sales of adult nappies growing year on year, futurist *Natalie D Kane* contemplates whether the diaper is a utopian or dystopian prospect.

Broach the subject of the adult nappy and it usually ends in a punchline. To mask our discomfort with the topic, manufacturers and marketers use language to deflect attention from the product's purpose and infantile associations; they entice the elderly to purchase nappies by using names such as 'protective underwear' and 'comfort solutions'. When equipping their operatives for missions that don't allow time for toilet breaks, the military-industrial complex swaps the mass-market's cosy platitudes for the rhetoric of efficiency. Heroes don't wear diapers: each Nasa astronaut leaves earth's orbit proudly sporting a 'Maximum Absorbency Garment'. Other products such as the 'Wellness Brief' bridge both worlds, boasting Nasa-inspired 'InconTek' technology to appeal to seniors who want the cutting edge.

Such semantic sleights of hand, and the anxieties they reveal, are significant in an age where going on-the-go is increasingly common. According to Euromonitor International, the nappy market for infants in the US is expected to increase only 2.6 percent by 2020. In the same time, the forecaster predicts a 48 percent increase in the sale of adult nappies – from US$1.8 billion last year to US$2.7 billion. The expansion of this industry is due to longer lifespans in many developed nations; the median age for Japan's population, for instance, is set to reach at least 53 by 2020. As a result, the country's adult diaper market is growing by six to ten percent each year. It is currently a 140 billion yen industry.

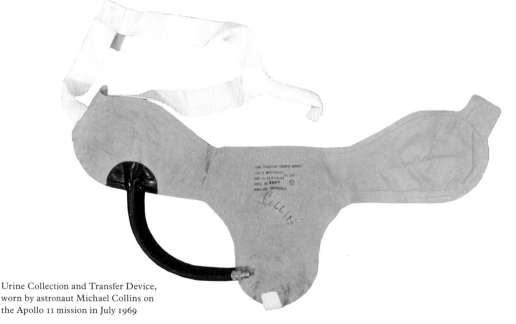

Urine Collection and Transfer Device,
worn by astronaut Michael Collins on
the Apollo 11 mission in July 1969

Aging Lifestyle Research Centre fashion show in Tokyo, September 25, 2008

For nappy brands, the elderly are an attractive target group. They combine ample disposable income with myriad care needs. The trick lies in how to reposition a product many find shameful so that it carries no stigma. This seemed to be the agenda of Tokyo's Aging Lifestyle Research Center, which, in 2008, held a fashion show to raise awareness of adult nappies. Models, dressed in black – to contrast with their white nappies – strutted the catwalk to the strains of the song *Relax* by Frankie Goes to Hollywood. The demonstration included a variety of nappy types, from those designed for the bedridden, to a lighter, more discrete, everyday version, signalling their potential for a range of ages. 'Diapers are something that people don't want to look at,' said the centre's Kiyoko Hamada. 'But if you make them attractive, then people can learn about them more easily.'

Making diapers desirable requires a certain level of design intervention, however, not just a change of context. This is a view shared by London-based graduate designer Stephanie Monty, who transformed a colostomy bag into an ornate prosthesis that can be worn on 'intimate occasions'. The prototype is intended to complement lingerie and the silicone can be colour-matched to the wearer's skin. 'There are over 250,000 ostomates in the UK alone and despite a wide range of highly advanced appliances, issues with their functionality and especially their aesthetics merely compound the social stigma surrounding this subject,' Monty explained.

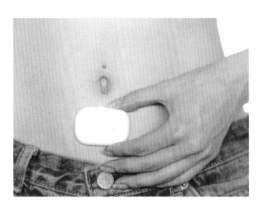

Triple W, D Free, 2015

Stephanie Monty, Colostomy Bag, 2016

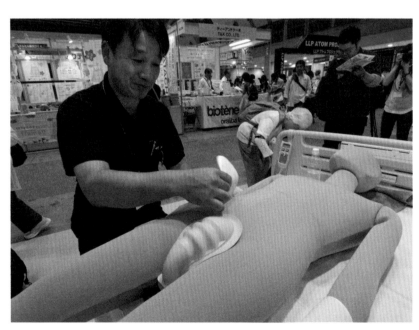

Muscle Corps, Robohelper, 2012

Indeed most nappies are extremely rudimentary single-use garments that rely on absorbent materials to collect and hold waste. They are often uncomfortable, have a tendency to leak and smell, and can cause a range of skin problems. Absorbency and fastenings have improved, but the nappy still leaves people standing in a bag of their own excrement. Even Nasa's nappies rely on this basic principle; they might be able to put a man on the moon, but they have yet to work out how to let him defecate with dignity. With the variety of prostheses available on the high street to augment consumers' other physical and mental capacities, it is remarkable that this most primordial function – defecation – has been overlooked.

There are some exceptions. The Dfree, a Japanese device that sits in your underwear and monitors your bowel movements, tallies well in a market flooded with health and fitness-focused wearables that micromanage many of our bodily functions – from how much protein you have eaten to how far you have walked. Though originally designed for those suffering from bowel disorders, it's not hard to envisage the Dfree being adopted by those who want to maximise their efficiency and rigorously plan their bowel movements. There's also Muscle Corps's Robohelper

They might be able to put a man on the moon, but they have yet to work out how to let him defecate with dignity.

Love, again intended for Japan's ageing population, which automatically removes waste while the user is asleep, taking a burden off carers and enabling the wearer to wake up clean. The device fastens between the legs and features a sensor attached to a suction mechanism that 'flushes' into a storage tank when it detects waste. The system then self-cleans.

If refined a little further, such advances in design may help to shift the perception of adult nappies beyond merely addressing the inadequacies of ageing or broken bodies. We could reimagine the nappy as a product which enhances human capability by enabling our independence from the bathroom, as much a drain on time as it is for waste. Could we, in fact, view the nappy as a component of an exciting, utopian ideal, whereby the restrictions placed on us by our body's dependence on grounded, immovable infrastructure are removed?

Considering the nappy as a form of personal infrastructure helps contextualise it in a lineage of radical mid-century architecture. For architects such as London-based Archigram, Austrian group Haus-Rucker-Co and Viennese architect Hans Hollein, personal mobile systems rather than inert monuments were essential to humanity's emancipation. The key to technological progress, these groups wrote, was to move. This culture of itinerancy, removing the anchor of 'place', was a reaction to the bombarded, broken cities after World War Two, and a step towards a new kind of workforce which moved where and when it was needed.

Archigram's Warren Chalk envisioned a technological society where 'people will play an active role in determining their own environment, in a self-determining way of life.' The group's *Cushicle*, for instance, was a speculative design for a complete environment that could be carried on a citizen's back, providing food, water, heating and entertainment. The inflatable carapace, with its exterior skin and interior matrix of plugs, power cables and apertures, clearly referenced biological structures. But this bodily metaphor stopped short of the anus. As with other mobile architecture propositions of the era, issues of waste management were largely ignored. Archigram's greatest champion, the architecture critic Reyner Banham, hinted at this last unavoidable link to the grid with his own idea of a mobile living unit, the 'Transportable Standard-of-Living Package'. A free-floating membrane, it allowed inhabitants to roam free and came complete with all the technical affordances one could wish for, that is, except for a connection to a 'brick-built bathroom unit'.

To a certain extent, the visions of those radical architects have been realised. Advances in communication technologies and decreases in the cost of international travel mean that, except for legal restrictions, we can live and work almost anywhere on the planet. Art collective Åyr's contribution to the British Pavilion at the 2016 Venice Architecture Biennale clearly shared the same preoccupation. Titled *Home is Where the Wifi is*, the installation comprised only two inflatable balls: portable shelters from which owners could conduct their digital lives. Much of Archigram's assistive technologies have been shrunk into the six inches of glass and metal most now carry in their pockets. What still remains conspicuously absent in these imaginings, however, is the toilet. Were architects to turn their attention to defecation they might find the missing piece of the puzzle.

But is this really what we want? Our era of unprecedented mobility has actually created conditions in which the nappy facilitates stasis and uninterrupted concentration. Recently, Amazon's 'recommendation' algorithm threw up a link between two disparate products: adult nappies and video game Call of Duty

Haus-Rucker-Co, *Mind Expander/Flyhead Helmet*, 1968

David Green, Archigram, inflatable suit-home (suit made by Pat Haines). 1968.
Suit inflated and being occupied as a home. This is a working model for the *Suitaloon*
project by Michael Webb, which was made for the Milan Triennale of 1968

Haus-Rucker-Co, *Oase No. 7*, Fridericianum, Documenta 5, Kassel 1972.

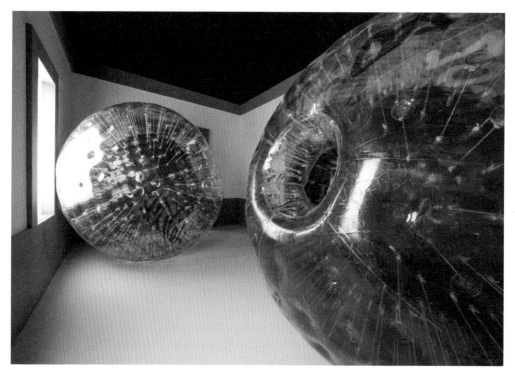

Åyr, *Home is Where the Wifi is*, British Pavilion, Venice Architecture Biennale 2016

Chicken-processing factory

appeared as 'frequently bought together', revealing the obsessive practices of the video game player, trading off toilet trips for a potential advantage in online multiplayer competitions. The use of adult diapers was also uncovered in Shosh Shlam and Hilla Medalia's documentary *China's Web Junkies*: 'Some kids are so hooked on games they think going to the bathroom will affect their performance. So they wear a diaper,' says a doctor working at one of the internet-addiction treatment centres that are the film's focus. 'The teenagers we have here crave and look forward to playing games online every day. That's why we call it electronic heroin.'

As these examples show, nappies fuel obsessive impulses, enabling people to override the metabolic demands of the human body. In 2007 astronaut Lisa Nowak drove nearly 1,000 miles from Houston to Orlando airport – allegedly wearing a nappy so she wouldn't have to stop – to attack a love rival. And in the realm of government, senators determined to push a motion forward will filibust – obstruct legislation – by talking at great length. How they do so has been the cause of much speculation. Senator Wendy Davis was thought to manage her eleven-hour stance against Texan abortion laws with the aid of a discretely fitted catheter, while Connecticut Senator Christopher Murphy was rumoured to use adult diapers during his fifteen-hour push for gun-law change.

Nappies aid feats of endurance. But serious problems arise when pressure not to take a toilet break comes from above.

Earlier this year, Oxfam released a report exposing the abhorrent conditions suffered by poultry workers at North Carolina's Tyson Foods factory, where the reported 'culture of fear' meant employees were forced to wear Pampers because they were afraid to ask permission for a toilet break. 'Nearly everyone has stories of workers peeing on the line,' the report stated. 'Still others make the choice to wear diapers to work. Others report that they stop drinking water and become dehydrated.' In a country where laws exist to protect employees from such treatment, taking full advantage of those rights in this particular case might come at the cost of one's job. Elsewhere, employers have made nappies mandatory to ensure efficiency. The Metropolitan Manila Development Authority insists that its traffic enforcers wear diapers, following the lead of Buckingham Palace guards, Nato soldiers and the US Army.

When individual employers are involved, it's obvious who is responsible. But how do you deal with paradigm shifts in the national economy of the world's most populous nation? China's mass rural-to-urban migration has created disparate family units that often live thousands of miles apart. On Lunar New Year, up to two billion Chinese migrant workers will make the pilgrimage home to celebrate with their families, leaving densely populated cities for outer regions. The transport infrastructure simply can't cope with the demand: trains become dangerously overcrowded, filled to over two hundred percent capacity, and passengers are forced to wear adult diapers to account for the lack of adequate waste management on board, contributing to a fifty percent rise in nappy sales.

'Filibuster' episode of NBC series *Parks and Recreation*

Photo by Bobby Yip © Reuters

Stranded train passengers wait outside a railway station in
China's southern city of Guangzhou February 1, 2008.

But it's not all bad. An unexpected outcome of the boom
in Japanese sales of adult diapers is the secondary infrastructure
that has appeared. Instead of contributing to landfill, fuel is now
generated from the shredded remains of the nappy, turning it into
bacteria-free pellets for use in stoves and biomass boilers, with a
hospital in Tokyo carrying out the first trial. Construction materials
are also derived from this by-product by companies such as Total
Care Systems, which turn the nappy waste collected from hospitals,
homes and care facilities into plastics and pulp.

It's easy to imagine China implementing a waste-disposal
system similar to Japan's in order to deal with the huge amount of
waste generated as desperate passengers make this journey home.
Rather than dealing with the cause of the problem directly, one can
foresee a secondary, potentially profitable, industry emerging. As is
often the case, the market intervenes not to correct a problem, but
to exploit it.

Most of these examples point to a fundamental failing in the
way things have been done at a macro level. Rather than beating
the system, and realising the dreams of the avant-garde architects,
we have instead become enmeshed in broken systems. How do we
react? We adapt our behaviour accordingly and take on the cost of
failed infrastructure ourselves. Should we really all wear nappies?

This essay inspired *On the Go*, an exhibition curated by
Dirty Furniture at the London Design Festival 2016.

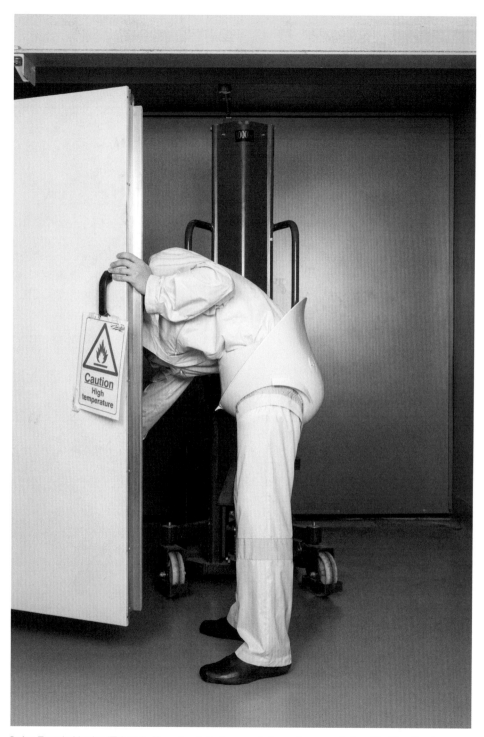

Lukas Franciszkiewicz (Takram), *Heavy Load*, 2016, a speculative project commissioned by *Dirty Furniture*

Narendra Modi wields a broom to launch *Swachh Bharat Abhiyan* in Valmiki Basti, New Delhi, 2014.

A National Blockage

Of the estimated 946 million people worldwide who don't use toilets, 564 million live in India. Journalist *Debika Ray* surveys the role design can play in dealing with the country's sanitation problem.

On 2 October 2014, India's prime minister Narendra Modi took to the streets of Delhi wielding a broom. With this stunt, he launched *Swachh Bharat Abhiyan* – the 'Clean India Mission' – to improve sanitary conditions across the country. The date was significant: it was the 145th birthday of India's founding father Mahatma Gandhi, who famously declared 'sanitation is more important than independence'. By 2019, what would have been Gandhi's 150th birthday, Modi has pledged to end outdoor defecation in India by building 120 million toilets.

Even opponents of Modi – a right-wing nationalist with a history of stoking community tensions – concede the worthiness of this goal. It is a goal, however, that successive governments since Gandhi have tried, but failed to realise. Swachh Bharat succeeded *Nirmal Bharat Abhiyan* (Pure India Campaign, 2012), which itself followed both the Total Sanitation Campaign (1999) and the Central Rural Sanitation Programme (1986). For his part, Modi has pledged US$29 billion, from a combination of private and public sources, towards building public and community toilets. He has also increased subsidies for families to build their own. This generous toilet spend is in part driven by a desire to improve India's poor international reputation for hygiene; this needs to be addressed if Modi is to meet his promise of economic reform through increased foreign investment.

Sadly, the reputation is not undeserved. India has the highest rate of outdoor defecation in the world: of the estimated 946 million people worldwide who don't use toilets, 564 million live there; that means almost half of India's population – including the majority of the 276 million people in India who live below the poverty line – defecates and urinates on railway tracks, in open fields, garbage dumps, parks and ditches. The health consequences of this are catastrophic. Almost four hundred children die every day from diarrhoea-related illness, while 38 percent of under-fives have their growth stunted as a result, with effects on long-term health and cognitive development. The costs of death, disease and water treatment in India as well as losses in education, productivity and tourism add up to US$53.8 billion a year.

The current government claims to have built at least eight million toilets since the campaign launched, but the initiative is not having the desired effect. A recent survey by the government's National Sample Survey Office conducted in 2015 found more than half of these toilets are sitting unused. A different study by Deloitte in 2013 revealed that approximately sixty percent of the subsidies offered under the previous campaign were not claimed. People continue to defecate outdoors.

So, why are these initiatives failing? While formal sewerage infrastructure is rare in many developing countries, affordable, off-grid latrines are commonplace; poorer countries – such as India's neighbour, Bangladesh – have made great strides in adopting them.

In India the question of whether one actually uses a toilet is influenced by a number of factors: if you are upper or lower class, high or low caste, educated or uneducated, male or female, urban- or rural-dwelling, living formally or informally. Authorities have barely begun to unpick these complexities. Their focus is numbers. They contract out much of the construction to private and part-private organisations with few clear instructions on design and build, beyond the fact that the toilets should 'have a substructure which is sanitary'. As such, what is often built is little more than a small, stuffy room with a pit underneath to collect waste.

If it's customisable

Indian architect Anupama Kundoo is a fierce critic of this quantitative approach. She has spent 25 years developing low-cost housing in India by engaging with local communities, and presented a prototype of a toilet at this year's Venice Biennale. She insists people are more likely to install – and use – a toilet if it's customisable.

To demonstrate this, she designed the modular Easy WC (2016) using ferrocement – a light, high-strength material that can be made by local masons simply by layering mortar or plaster over metal mesh. 'When people typically design a toilet with brick, cement, tiles and pipes, you need to build foundations, bring in plumbers, masons, electricians – it can take a month,' she says. Kundoo's design can be assembled in two days by unskilled workers. Seven prefabricated elements fit together to form a toilet and shower on either side of a covered platform. The main component is the base, a floor pre-fitted with a squat or seated toilet that plugs directly into one of three sanitation systems: a septic tank (a self-contained waste-treatment unit Kundoo plans to offer in prefabricated form), an underground pit or a formal sewage system.

So far, Kundoo has built two prototypes. She has yet to test them (beyond using them in her studio), but she is confident of the design's potential – primarily because she has drawn, not on research into toilets, but her work on site with rural and low-income groups in India. Like her Full Fill Home (2015), a modular, quick-to-build, flexible house, the Easy WC aims to give people who would otherwise have solutions imposed upon them control over their environment. It respects their right to have preferences, and

Anupama Kundoo, *Easy WC*, 2016

crucially, participate in making an environment that is pleasant to be in. It's a mistake, she says, to assume that poor people don't care about this: 'People think a poor person will put up with any shitty solution. It's not true.' In Kundoo's toilet design, light and ventilation are ample and because the system is modular, the walls, roof and doors are optional: 'You don't need to invest in the whole structure – the sanitation component is a must, but above ground you can just use a curtain for privacy...You can have [the toilet] open to the air for as long as you want.'

Here, Kundoo refers to an important and often overlooked issue: the widespread unease in India with using indoor toilets. The Squat Report, a 2014 research initiative in north India by the non-profit, Research Institute for Compassionate Economics (Rice), found that forty percent of rural households with a working latrine had at least one member who continued to defecate outdoors – and that almost half did so because they found it more 'pleasant, comfortable or convenient'. In fact, many said defecating in the open provided them an opportunity to take a walk, tend to their fields, take in fresh air, smoke and socialise; others said it was habit or tradition. It is also linked, in part, to religious belief.

Sulabh International, two-pit latrine, 2015

In many Hindu communities, there's a sense that toilets –
and the activities that take place inside them – should be located
as far from the home as possible. To a degree, this is down to the
legacy of the religion's caste system. According to traditional Hindu
social stratification, tasks like cleaning toilets and handling waste
were the job of people with the lowest social status, the so-called
'untouchables'. Higher-caste Hindus could only remain 'pure' if
they maintained distance from such people, and associated spaces
and activities. The result today is that many Indians are reluctant
to clean toilets or handle waste-disposal systems: upper-caste Hindus
because they consider it degrading and Dalits (the descendants of
'untouchables') because it's directly associated with their subjugation.
This attitude is reflected in the differences between Hindu and
Muslim communities: rates of open defecation are much higher
in Hindu households, although Muslims tend to be poorer and
less educated.

And this phenomenon influences the choices made by many
rural families when installing toilets. For example, in pit latrines – a
common toilet system for areas with no networked sewage facilities –
waste is deposited in an underground container that is either emptied

or replaced when full. A basic latrine with a pit of about fifty cubic feet can cost as little as 3,000 rupees (£30), but respondents to Rice's survey revealed they wanted latrines with pits twenty times this size – at a cost of 21,000 rupees each – so they wouldn't have to empty them as often. The Squat Report also found that pits built by households were on average 392 cubic feet, four times larger than the average 92-foot government-built pits, and that people who owned government-built toilets were more than twice as likely to defecate outdoors than those who built their own.

Findings such as this are uncomfortable, linked, as they are, to the legacy of the caste system – which the government has tried for decades to stamp out through legislation and affirmative action – but they are findings that can't be ignored. They point to the social issues around toilets, which must be considered when designing them. One solution is to develop systems that minimise human contact with waste or transform faecal matter into a less offensive form. Septic tanks treat waste, but they can be expensive and hazardous if improperly built and not serviced. The Indian government's Defence Research and Development Establishment has built a range of bio-toilets, which use bacteria to reduce waste to biogas and water (these have been installed on military bases, but are yet to be rolled out further). And there are plenty of blue-sky ideas. The Bill and Melinda Gates Foundation's Reinvent the Toilet Challenge has seen universities around the world use solar power and UV light to transform waste into fertiliser, electricity and charcoal. Important as this kind of research is, in reality, such solutions are expensive and complex. Spending 21,000 rupees to provide the larger, desired pits for the 123 million households that lack a toilet would cost almost US$40 billion, far too much to be a serious option.

Diagram of Nano Membrane
Toilet, part of the Bill and
Melinda Gates Reinvent the
Toilet Challenge

Julia King, Decentralised Sanitation in Savda Ghevra Resettlement Colony, New Delhi, 2015

And yet, such high-tech solutions aren't always necessary. Charity Sulabh International has built more than a million twin-pit latrines in India since the 1970s. Simply put, this design has two pits that are used alternately. When one is full, waste is directed to the second, while the sludge in the first dries to become odourless, dry, and pathogen free. In the charity's experience, there is less aversion to handling excreta in this form.

'It's not that we don't have the techniques to deal with poo – there are plenty of solutions,' says British-Venezuelan architect Julia King. King works on housing and sanitation projects in Delhi with the Indian NGO Centre for Urban and Regional Excellence (Cure). The projects they take on are site-specific, and the solution is always different. One of the most significant was at Savda Ghevra, a resettlement colony not connected to sewage infrastructure, on the edge of Delhi. Here, the team retrofitted a sanitation system to 322 pre-existing houses (each different), to provide the households with a private toilet. As the plots were too small to treat effluent on site, each toilet was connected to a communal septic tank, linked to a decentralised treatment system which treated the effluent before discharging it.

'A lot of the work I do is very basic in terms of the technology and design,' says King. It's something she's come under criticism for. At a recent conference about innovation, King encountered a baffled audience member who told her there was nothing innovative about her work. '"Yes," I responded, "my great grandfather was building these systems in Venezuela and I've used ideas from projects done in the 1970s",' she says. 'The architectural intervention is as much about getting a truck through a narrow lane, navigating informal settlements, figuring out how to finance a project.' But impressive as King's work is, she can't solve the problem single-handedly. A hands-on role from the government, and greater investment in sewage infrastructure are needed: 'When it comes to the installation of basic services, it's a gross miscalculation to imagine the private sector is going to fix it. We need the state to intervene – and on the ground, not from a computer.'

Julia King, Decentralised Sanitation in Savda Ghevra Resettlement Colony, New Delhi, 2015

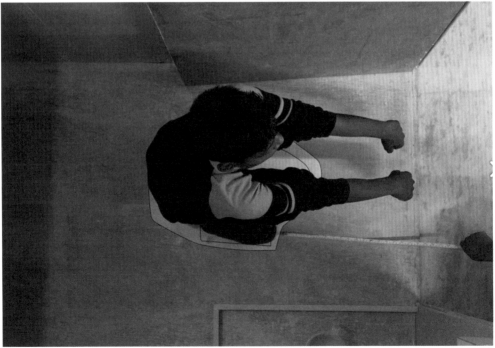

Developing designs for Project Sammaan's shared facilities in Orissa

Five hundred people who need to use the toilet

'On the ground' is key because to succeed in ending outdoor defecation, human needs and preferences have to be taken into consideration – and this can't be achieved without dialogue. The Swachh Bharat guidelines, for example, suggest building communal toilet complexes where there is a lack of space for household toilets, but the Squat Report reveals a deep aversion in rural areas to sharing toilets, so efforts to build community facilities there are arguably misguided. Kundoo despairs: 'You can't offer people a shared toilet as their only option, then say toilets are failing. The disgust for public toilets has to be acknowledged.' (She believes her Easy WC could be built at a low enough cost to be a viable alternative to community toilets, and that it's compact enough for cities too.)

For now though shared facilities are likely to remain part of public sanitation policy in dense, urban areas. Fortunately, urban Indians do not share their rural counterparts' ingrained aversion to indoor defecation. Needs must, and 'in cities, it's much harder to find a field to poo in,' says King.

The problem is the condition of many toilet blocks. Rarely serviced, they quickly fall into disrepair. There is another basic problem: 'Most people will poo before they go to work, so you get five hundred people who need to use the toilet in a 45-minute timeframe – no infrastructure could take that,' says King.

Here, again, the answer is not about high-end design and technology. Design consultancy Quicksand has been running Project Sammaan – an initiative to develop public and community sanitation facilities in two cities in eastern India – since 2012, based on the findings of the Potty Project, a study funded by the Gates Foundation on user behaviour in public toilets. Queues, for example, are inevitable, but Project Sammaan's toilets are designed with facilities that can be used while you wait, such as a spit trough to brush your teeth. 'People tend to defecate or urinate first, then bathe, so that's how our interiors were designed,' says Quicksand's spokesperson Kevin Shane. 'It's hoped this will lead to less time within the facilities and reduce waiting times.' Automated payment interfaces and more centrally located caretaker's booths mean greater opportunity for supervision, so generally cleaner facilities. User fees are another area for experimentation: reduced pricing during off-peak hours can help spread out use more evenly, while a fee itself can make people more conscious about keeping a facility clean. Community-managed facilities, where people have a sense of ownership, tend to be better maintained than privately or government-managed ones, Shane says. There were even instances in which specific stalls were allocated to a certain number of families – this was effective because they felt more accountable for maintenance.

No Toilet, No Bride

Many communal toilets don't have separate areas for women or, if they do, it's an exact replica of the male section. 'We provided gender-segregated areas designed to account for individual needs, including a menstrual waste incinerator in the women's section,' Shane says. 'We also included full doors on our stalls and separate entrances for women and men to help avoid instances of harassment.'

Here Shane touches on one of the most contentious issues regarding outdoor defecation. 'Women suffer the most,' says Ranjana Kumari, director of the Centre for Social Research, an NGO focused on women's empowerment. While men can relieve themselves outdoors with relative freedom, women are at risk of sexual assault when defecating or managing their menstrual hygiene, particularly when travelling to secluded spots during hours of darkness in an effort to be discreet. 'They have to go to the fields before sunrise or after sunset, with no chance between, even if they are ill,' says Kumari. The lack of toilets in schools, she adds, means girls frequently drop out of education when they start menstruating.

As women are rarely household decision-makers or community spokespeople, empowering women is vital. This is the thinking behind 'No Toilet, No Bride', a government-backed campaign in the northern state of Haryana that seeks to educate women about toilet hygiene and persuade them to take a stand in favour of toilets. Kumari, whose NGO is involved, explains: 'We've been working to get young women to insist there is a toilet in their [prospective] in-laws' house before they agree to get married or to tell their parents not to let them marry into a house without a toilet.' It is hoped that such efforts will empower women to stand together and demand change in the face of India's patriarchal norms, and Kumari says there have been 'sporadic stories of success'. In any case, she senses a slow change, as India develops as a nation, because 'young women are now more educated, and more able to assert themselves in rural areas.'

Orissa State Water and Sanitation Mission billboard promoting 'No Toilet No Bride' campaign. Written in Oriya, the language of Orissa in eastern India.

Project Sammaan, addressing needs of shared facilities

Photo by Rose George, 2007 from her book *The Big Necessity: Adventures in the World of Human Waste*

A library of images

It's a sentiment echoed by Lakshmi Murthy, a communication
designer based in the northern state of Rajasthan, who has
worked for almost thirty years promoting better hygiene practices
among lesser-educated communities. Her work is vital because
it is education, ultimately, that all parties point to as crucial in
changing attitudes. The Squat Report indicates the preference
for open defecation is embedded in a lack of understanding about
its dangers: more than half of respondents who poo outdoors
were unaware it could be more damaging to child health than
latrine use.

To tackle this, Murthy designs communications targeted
to specific groups. For more informed urban audiences, 'you can
show horrific visuals and tell them flies will sit on shit and then
on food,' she says, but in other cases, it isn't that simple. Women,
for example, must be targeted specifically; they may not be
invited to gatherings with village decision makers. And pictorial
communication is fundamental for reaching illiterate groups.
In the past, Murthy has engaged with locals to create a library
of images relevant to the rural environment through drawing
workshops. She discovered a collective consciousness behind
rural signs, and was able to use this to develop a visual system of
codes, building picture dictionaries specific to different locations.
Even in the time Murthy has developed this strategy, her work has

Adolescent girls at a training programme using the menstrual wheel.

Lakshmi Murthy and Jatan Sansthan's *Uger Project*, 2011.
The wheel describes the process of menstruation and is used as a training aid.

become easier. Thanks to improved infrastructure, mobile phones, televisions and new media 'more girls can now read,' she says. There has also been a societal shift: 'Families were afraid to send their adolescent girls to our meetings, but this has changed too.'

The Squat Report concluded with a call for a widespread communications campaign about the importance of latrine use, led at the top by respected public figures and on the ground by local government workers with connections to the communities. Murthy confirms that such messages are better received when delivered by people known in the community than by outsiders. Modi has listened – but selectively. He has enlisted several high-profile individuals to help spread the word including former cricketer Sachin Tendulkar and veteran Bollywood actor Amitabh Bachchan. But, much to the surprise of many, the Swachh Bharat campaign also halved spending on information, education and communication to just eight percent of the total budget.

With such cuts, where should the designer concentrate his or her attention now? Perhaps, suggest Murthy and Kundoo, they should focus on doing what they usually do quite well. Beyond educating people, Murthy and Kundoo argue that the toilet needs to be sought after as an aspirational product – like mobile phones or motorcycles – both of which are common in rural areas. 'A motorcycle is a status symbol, but a toilet is not, so it's not a priority,' says Murthy. Kundoo agrees, 'Toilets should be popularised and marketed like they are a cool thing – just like a cell phone is – perhaps by introducing demo models then giving people incentives to try them out.' Ultimately, real change depends on people wanting toilets – not having toilets imposed upon them.

Subscribe to Dirty Furniture

Order the annual 6-issue set for £55*

Got an issue already?
Complete your set for £44*

*Get one issue free

~~Table~~   ~~Couch~~

Bed   Telephone

~~Toilet~~   Closet

www.dirty-furniture.com